AÏR
MOUNTAINS

NIGER

CHAD

I

R. Niger

PER
LTA

Lake
Chad

REPUBLIC
OF
B
GERMANTOWN FRIENDS SCHOOL LIBRARY

TOGO

A

NIGERIA

BAUCHI
PLATEAU

R. Benue

R. Niger

CAMEROUN MOUNTAINS

CAMEROUN

EQUATORIAL
GUINEA

GABON

Black
Kingdoms
Black
Peoples

Black Kingdoms Black Peoples

The West African Heritage

Anthony Atmore and
Gillian Stacey

Photographs by
Werner Forman

G. P. Putnam's Sons · New York

Front endpaper: Contemporary political/physical map of West Africa.

Back endpaper: Historical map of West Africa.

Half-title page: Janus-type headdress made by the Idoma of Nigeria. The male element is on the left, the female on the right.

Title page: Edan Ogboni society staffs; cultic instruments connected with divination in relation to, for example, healing. The staffs are usually joined by a chain, parts of which can be seen in the picture. On the left is the male, holding a miniature image of an Edan Ogboni, and on the right the female, giving the secret sacred greeting of the left fist over right with both thumbs covered.

This page: Upper Guinea miniature mask used by secret societies as a recognition feature, decorated with cowrie shells.

SBN 399-12254-0
Library of Congress Catalog Card Number 78-71755
Printed in Italy by IGDA, Novara

Contents

Introduction

I call Gold, Gold is mute.
I call Cloth, Cloth is mute.
It is Mankind that matters.

(Anon., Gold Coast, eighteenth century)

The Land of Blacks, the Land of Gold, the Land of Slaves—for centuries West Africa was a mystery to the outside world, known only for the colour of its peoples' skins, its fabulous mineral wealth and the seemingly endless supply of strong young men and women that could be taken from its shores to a life of forced labour. Those who looked closer at this unknown land found a galaxy of cultures so varied and so different from anything they had known before that they were baffled by its complexities.

Today there are more than 130 million people living in West Africa, in an area stretching from the Atlantic coast of Mauritania and Senegal in the west to Lake Chad and Mount Cameroun in the east. Although the region has been divided into some fifteen modern nation states, the diversity of cultures remains staggering. Nigeria alone has more than 300 quite distinct ethnic groups, speaking almost as many different languages. A Fulani cattleman in the north of the country feels he has little in common with a Yoruba bureaucrat in the Nigerian capital.

Yet just as the peoples of Europe recognize some indefinable quality which is 'European' and which binds them together, so there is an underlying character which is West African. Over the centuries up to colonial times, these many cultures have been woven into a tapestry of endless different colours, designs and pictures—a tapestry with a uniqueness and a grandeur of its own. It is marked with a profound African humanism, coupled with a realistic appraisal of the material aspects of life:

'Then they said that God did give unto them no gold but the earth did give it unto them wherein they did seek it and find it out. Nor did God give unto them neither millet nor corn but the earth did give it unto them when they did sow it and afterwards at the right time did reap and garner it. And for the fruits, these the trees did give unto them which they themselves had planted . . . The young goats or lambs did come from the old ones. The sea did give unto them fishes and they needs must catch them therein . . . These things did come not from God but were brought forth from the earth and from the water and were gained by their labour.' (Report by G. A. von Dantzig, 1603, quoted in J. Jahn *Muntu* London 1961)

Yet this down-to-earth appreciation that it is the soil and their own human toil which will provide men with their daily bread is but one side of the West African coin. The other is the world of spirit, as real as the red earth of their homeland and a part of everyday life. There is no rigid division between men, spirits and gods as there is in other parts of the world. Fashioning an ornament of gold or even planting the new year's crops involve both human craftsmanship and labour, and participation in the spiritual world of magic—typical of the constant West African combination of materialism and utilitarianism on the one hand with the working of a spiritual dimension on the other.

Human responses like fear, awe and reverence are given a supernatural or independent existence with powers to intervene in human affairs. For example, laughter can become a pervasive force, with the ability to mitigate suffering, meanness, misery and monotony, and will be seen as an independent being: 'We knew Laugh personally on that night, because as every one of them stopped laughing at us on that night, my wife and myself forgot our pains and laughed with him, because he was laughing with curious voices that we never heard before in our life' (A. Tutuola *The Palm-Wine Drunkard* London 1952).

Similarly, the ties that unite matter with the spirits link the living and the dead. Death is merely a transition, not an end or a barrier: a community of people consists of the unborn, the living and the dead.

On page 6 : The Atlantic coast of Ghana, with gathering storm clouds. This is the zone of tropical forests, which experience almost daily rainfall.

Below : Soapstone head known as Mahanyate, found in north-eastern Sierra Leone and central Guinea. Such heads were associated with the fertility rites of the Kru and Mende peoples of the region.

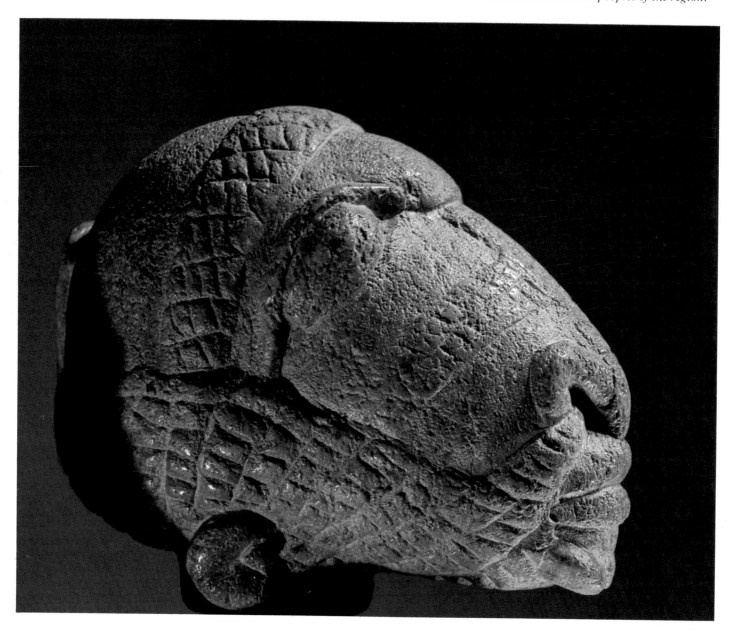

'Those who are dead are never gone,
    they are in the breast of the woman,
    they are in the child who is wailing,
    and in the firebrand that flames.
    The dead are not under the earth;
    they are in the fire that is dying,
    they are in the grasses that weep,
    they are in the whimpering rocks,
    they are in the forest, they are in the house,
    the dead are not dead.'
        (Birago Diop, trans. by J. Jahn *Muntu* London 1961)

Ritual, dance, masks and laughter all belong to this realm of transition, where matter and spirit meet. The well-being and goodwill of the dead are vital to the fecundity and happiness, let alone the survival, of the living. Death and life are interchangeable, immutable; the one can elevate the other. Nature and spirit, flesh, blood and ghosts, these are the ingredients of the mystery, the drama of West African life. And for all its spiritual dimension, it is deeply human and humanistic.

This drama is set on an immense stage, a land as large as the United States, but entirely within the tropics. To the north the Sahara Desert, and to the south the Atlantic Ocean form massive backdrops, always influencing and sometimes controlling the action. From the Sahara comes a hot, dry and dusty mass of air which, when it blows up into a strong wind, is known in Arabic as the *Harmattan*. Opposing this, a warm, moist air mass formed over the southern Atlantic comes inland from July to December, bringing rains to most parts of West Africa. In this country of extremes, the lands bordering the desert get little or no rain, while parts of the seaboard have an almost continual downpour. But if the annual battle is not fought out, or if the Harmattan should win, the result is widespread drought, a real and terrible tragedy for millions of people.

Soil and climate have always governed the lives of West Africans to a very high degree: indeed, it was the combination of the two that brought some at least of their ancestors into the region more than 5,000 years ago. At that time the Sahara was not the desert it is now but a region of well-watered grasslands and woods, much like the savannah further south today. The numerous and beautiful rock paintings found there show that the Sahara was inhabited by both Negroes and Caucasians, and that cattle and wild animals provided a stable source of food. But as the climate changed and the Sahara became dessicated, the black men moved south to mix with other Negro peoples already living in West Africa.

Some two to three thousand years ago, these Stone Age peoples, who were probably living mainly along the banks of rivers and lake shores, gathering wild vegetables and fruit and catching fish, began to cultivate tropical crops such as millet, sorghum and yams. Some, especially those who moved south from the Sahara, remained nomadic, raising cattle, sheep and goats. But where crops grew plentifully and the fishing was good, or where game could be hunted, populations multiplied.

Knowledge of iron-making techniques spread south from the Mediterranean in the last centuries BC. New, stronger tools made it much easier to clear trees and scrub, as well as to dig the ground, so far more land could be brought under cultivation. Most of the major cultural achievements of the West African people date from the introduction of iron, as does the foundation of the great empires and lesser kingdoms, which seem to have developed first in the areas immediately to the south of the Sahara, and then moved further south into the savannahs and forests.

The Sahara was to remain a major feature in the rise and fall of African dynasties and empires. Until the first cautious voyage of the Portuguese mariners in the fifteenth century the desert was the only means of approach to the region, and it was only across the Sahara that West Africans had any contact with the outside world. It was with the coming of the Arabs in the

Above : The Sahel in Niger. Lying between the Sahara and the savannah grasslands, the arid Sahel forms the northern side of West Africa.

9

seventh century that the desert was opened up to international trade, which, together with soil and climate, was to be one of the major determinants of West African life. As Fez and Marrakesh and other towns of the *Maghrib* (the Arabic name for north-west Africa) grew rich, the Arabs dug wells and maintained tracks in the desert which made it easier for travellers to cross it. The streets of the principal ports of the Maghrib, from Ceuta in the west to Tripoli in the east, became thronged with Italian and Sicilian traders, eager for business with their Arab counterparts. They came not only for the wheat and fruit which grew in profusion on the plains of Ifriqiya (the Arabic name for modern Tunisia, from the Latin name Africa), but for the burgeoning trans-Saharan gold trade with the Land of Blacks, *Bilad as-Sudan*.

Despite the oases, crossing the desert remained a perilous undertaking, and it was probably only the fact that the trade was in gold that provided the incentive. A medieval traveller, Ibn Battuta, left a vivid account of his crossing in 1352. First he waited with a caravan at Sijilmasa, an oasis city on the northern edge of the desert in the foothills of the High Atlas, where he bought camels and foddered them for four months until the end of the rainy season. Finally, when the watering places were full and there was still some pasture for the animals, they were led out by Berber guides, who were essential as blown sand quickly obscured any tracks. When one trader in the caravan lagged behind he was lost forever. The column marched until the sun was high in the sky, then rested and set off again in late afternoon until some time after nightfall.

The journey from oasis to oasis was slow, and then came a stretch where there was no water at all. When the water-skins were empty, camels were slaughtered for the water in their stomachs. Now the caravan began the daily march in the afternoon and travelled throughout the night until sunrise. At last a guide was sent on to the oasis of Walata to announce their impending arrival. If one of the crucial watering places had dried up or been poisoned by desert tribesmen, the whole caravan was likely to perish. But carriers from Walata finally appeared with four days' supply of water and the exhausted travellers struggled onwards. Altogether the journey had lasted two months.

Walata was situated on the southern border of the desert, and, like Timbuktu on the Niger further to the east, was a busy, bustling town, a trading centre from which goods could be gathered and dispersed throughout West Africa. To the Arabs it seemed like a port, and the region at the edge of the desert they likened to the shores of an ocean, naming it *Sahel*. The Sahel belt of dry grasslands runs from the Atlantic coast around the mouth of the Senegal river to beyond Lake Chad—a flat, featureless expanse broken only by the occasional thorn bush or tree. It is the home of camel and cattle nomads—the Tuareg and Fulani—as well as of scattered farmers, all living a precarious existence at the mercy of a fickle climate.

Further south were grasslands where the soil was more fertile, the water supplies more frequent and dependable. This area became known as the *Sudan* after the Arab term for Black people, a name which should not be confused with the modern state of the same name. Rich farming land produced harvests good enough to sustain large populations, and it was the cities of the Sudan that provided the main demand for Arab trade. Some exchange of gold and kola for salt, clothes and luxury goods took place in the Sahel, but for the most part the bulk goods of the caravans were broken down into smaller loads and sent to places such as Jenné, for long one of the most important trading cities in the whole of West Africa.

Jenné lies on the Bani river, a tributary of the Niger, the great river which flows through the Sudan in a vast spreading arc, a highway for every variety of river traffic. At the crown of the arc, around Timbuktu, the Niger flows through desert lands, but merchants travelling upstream from Timbuktu in canoes paddled by professional Bambara watermen witnessed extraordinary changes in scenery. Soon after leaving Timbuktu they would enter an immense inland delta formed by innumerable tributaries and

Above : A rock engraving from Tamaron, East Air, northern Nigeria, dating from 5488–2780 BC, and now deep in the Sahara. Pastoral people grazed their cattle on grasslands when the Sahara was much wetter than in historic times.

Left : A cave at Koroun Korokale in south-western Mali, where many Stone Age implements have been found dating from some two thousand years ago.

Below: Life-size pottery head from Nok, Nigeria. Nok culture flourished between 500 BC and AD 200.

Above : Bambara marionette or puppet used as a cult figure by professional entertainers near the Niger river in Mali.

Right : Part of the city of Jenné, on the Bani river, a tributary of the Niger. Jenné, an important trading centre, was mud built, as were all the towns and cities of the Sudanic zone.

Below : A soapstone head, probably used in fertility rites in Sierra Leone.

lakes and swamps, the basin of a great inland lake which dried up several thousand years ago. On either side of the wide main stream the vegetation became luxuriant—high banks of reeds, elephant grass and papyrus, and beyond these thick bushes and trees or verdant meadows on which grazed great herds of wild animals. For the final stretch of the journey from Timbuktu to Jenné goods would be transferred on to donkeys and carried through the lush grasslands to the walled city.

This is savannah country, where some of the greatest West African empires were founded. Enterprising kings of Ghana, Mali and Songhay had drained some of the swamps, cut canals to expedite river transport and laid out irrigation schemes to bring still more land under cultivation. But trade remained the life-blood of these empires, and at Jenné as elsewhere in the western part of the Sudanic belt travellers would meet Mande-speaking Dyula people, who brought gold from the mining areas further south to exchange for salt and other goods carried across the Sahara.

From Jenné to Akan, hundreds of kilometres to the south, there is an even greater change in scenery. At first the savannah is gentle and passable but then becomes clustered with thick woods and bushes while remaining flat. The thick woodland savannah is plagued by the tsetse fly, which spreads sleeping sickness. Even humans can be infected, and many travellers would suffer frequent and unpleasant bouts of sickness and malaria the further south they journeyed.

This part of the country, known as the Guinea belt, stretches from the coast of Sierra Leone and Liberia across the two Volta rivers to the lower Niger and Benue. There are some hot, dry patches, but it is mostly quite well watered, with fertile grasslands and dense woods. The Guinea belt also contains some of West Africa's few highland ranges: the Futa Jallon in the west, the Jos Plateau in Nigeria and the Cameroun mountains in the far south-east. These lands were inhabited by an extraordinary variety of peoples, such as the Bambara, the Senufo and most notably the Baule, who had lavish, strange—and at times frightening—religious customs. Vigorous dancers, they used bizarre masks and were excellent wood-carvers and sculptors. Most of these peoples lived in small, independent kingdoms.

East of Jenné the terrain is equally varied. Mountainous country rises below the Niger bend, providing the home of the Dogon, a proud, independent people who resisted all attempts to conquer them by a succession of empires. Famous for their dancing and their sculpture, their individuality was made still more emphatic by the design of their villages, which reflect their kinship relationships. More remarkable still was the way they disposed of their dead, by placing their corpses in caves high up in the cliffs above the villages—cliffs that are sheer and appear unclimbable.

South of Dogon country are the lands of a famous warrior people, the Mossi, in modern north Ghana and southern Upper Volta. To the west are the wooded savannah lands of the Nupe and the Ilorin. Fertile open savannah stretches though the mighty Yoruba empire of Oyo, far to the south of the Bilad as-Sudan, ending only in a great vegetational belt of tropical rain forest. In the forest, just to the west of the Niger delta, was the great kingdom of Benin. The rain forest ranges across West Africa stretching from Liberia in the west to the Cameroun mountains in the east. It is broken only in one region, between the modern cities of Accra and Lagos, where savannah country comes right down to the sea shore.

From Benin it was a short distance through dense mangrove swamps to reach the Atlantic. Between the mangrove swamps of Benin and the sandy shores of Ghana, where Atlantic rollers break relentlessly for hundreds of kilometres, lies a strange line of lagoons, one leading to another. There are few harbours and landing is dangerous; sandbars block access to the lagoons. There are few islands off the coast and even the slight variations in West Africa's 3,200 kilometre (2,000 mile) coastline did not lure fishermen far out into the ocean. So West Africans for the most part have been a land-based people, with their sights and aspirations directed firmly towards the interior.

Trade, migrations of people, and access to fertile agricultural areas determined the development of West African societies. Alongside the indivisibility of natural and spiritual life which pervades all West African societies can be discerned a division between the peoples of the north of the area and those of the south. North of a line from modern Gambia, through Upper Volta and the middle of Nigeria are the states, roughly, of the open savannah. These were generally formed earlier and were more affected by Islam. South of the line, in wooded savannah, are states like Oyo, Asante and Dahomey (and, in the forest, Benin) which were scarcely touched by Islam, and whose history became closely connected with European slaving and other trading activities.

The overall picture is one of diversity and unity—a diversity occasioned by geographical differences, the differences between nomads and farmers, traders and townsmen. But there is also a strong unity formed by the West African dependence on the land and climate. Living at one with nature, West Africans have evolved a deep relationship with their environment which they express in a multitude of ways; a response to life that is utterly different from the Christian and Muslim civilizations of the Mediterranean lands. For West Africans, their natural and spiritual lives are one and indivisible, and this results in a quality of life, a sense of humour and a sense of horror that are quite unique.

Above: The outstanding features of Dogon country are the massive cliffs of the escarpment separating the upland plateau from the plains below. Many of these cliffs are sheer, but the Tellem, who lived here before the Dogon, somehow gained access to the caves in them. Even today, the Dogon can reach only a few of these caves.

Right: Portuguese knights carved around an ivory salt-cellar dating from the sixteenth century, in a style related to Benin art. The Portuguese navigators first reached Benin in 1486. It is possible that this salt-cellar was made in Portugal, by African craftsmen taken there, either as freemen or as slaves. The prominent crossing of the dagger handle in the knight's belt could be deliberate, as the Benin were initially very impressed by Portuguese men and rendered everything about their appearance with great attention to detail.

The Kingdoms
of the North

The Carthaginians unlade their wares, and having disposed them after an orderly fashion along the beach, leave them, and, returning aboard their ships, raise a great smoke. The natives, when they see the smoke, come down to the shore, and, laying out to view so much gold as they think the worth of the wares, withdraw to a distance. The Carthaginians upon this come ashore and look. If they think the gold enough, they take it and go their way; but if it does not seem to them sufficient, they go aboard ship once more and wait patiently. Then the others approach and add to their gold, till the Carthaginians are content.

(Herodotus *History*)

Left : Guardians at the main gate of the palace of the Sultan of Agades, an oasis city of the Sahara, in the northern part of Niger. It used to be an important staging post on one of the great trans-Saharan trade routes, from Hausaland to North Africa. In those days, Agades was an independent sultanate, inhabited first by Hausa who migrated southwards to found the earliest city states, and then by Tuareg, the veiled camel nomads of the desert.

The gateway to West Africa for the outside world, until the Portuguese voyages of discovery in the fifteenth and sixteenth centuries, was the Maghrib—north-west Africa—and the Sahara Desert. The inhabitants of the Maghrib were Berber people, who lived as peasant farmers and herdsmen in the coastal plains and mountains of the High Atlas, and as nomads based on the oases of the Sahara. Mediterranean peoples, such as the Carthaginians, traded along the Atlantic coast of Morocco and even of Mauritania as early as the fifth century BC, using the system of 'dumb barter' described by Herodotus for their dealings. After their defeat of the Carthaginians, the Romans incorporated much of the Maghrib into their empire. The Romans made occasional sorties into the Sahara, and possibly to the lands of the blacks beyond, but it was not until the introduction of the camel from Asia at the end of the Roman period that travel across the terrible desert really became feasible. After the Arabs conquered the Maghrib in the seventh century AD, contacts across the desert became more frequent. The Berber desert tribesmen the Sanhaja and Tuareg, became dependent upon camels. Living in tents made from camelhair and wearing black veils to protect their faces from the biting winds and blowing sands, the fierce Berber nomads travelled great distances to graze their animals. They became expert in conducting the caravans across the desert, and some became traders in their own right. The demands of the great cities of the Arab and Mediterranean worlds for African products created an intense international commercial network across the Sahara between the Maghrib and West Africa.

Several products crossed the desert to satisfy the requirements of the Mediterranean lands, but of these gold was by far the most important. It was valued for its beauty, for use in ornaments and regalia, but above all as the metal used in coinage. The minting of gold coins was originally the exclusive prerogative of the Caliph of the early Muslim Empire, but by the ninth century the Islamic world was split up and several independent caliphs, including those in North Africa and Spain, struck their own gold dinars. From the thirteenth century the Italian city states also used a gold standard, and they were followed in this by the kingdoms in Christian Spain and other parts of Europe. There thus arose a pressing demand for gold, which could be met only from the fields of West Africa.

In exchange, West Africans valued all kinds of luxury goods and cloths, but the thing they needed most urgently was salt. In humid, tropical climates, body salt is lost rapidly through perspiration and must be replaced. There were few sources of local supply in West Africa, and most of the salt obtainable was mined in the Sahara, at places like Zaghaza and Taodeni, and then transported in solid bars over great distances by the Berber traders. Leo Africanus, a sixteenth-century Arab traveller, described the sorry condition of the miners in the desert:

> 'These workmen are all strangers, who sell the salt which they dig unto certain merchants that carry the same upon camels to the kingdom of Timbuktu, where there would otherwise be extreme scarcity of salt. Neither have the said diggers of salt, the slaves of the Mesufa tribe, any victuals but such as the merchants bring unto them, dates imported from Dra'a and Sijilmasa, camel's flesh and millet imported from the Negrolands. They are distant from all inhabited places almost twenty days' journey, insomuch that oftentimes they perish for lack of food, when as the merchants come not in due time unto them.' (*History and Description of Africa* trans. J. Pory and R. Brown, London 1896)

The social consequences of trading were much the same in Africa as anywhere in the world. Surpluses to actual requirements had to be extracted—the meat, hides or fruit exchanged for the special goods—and this could generally be done only through the emergence of a ruling group that would force the ordinary people to produce more than their immediate needs. In the Sudan, the introduction of agriculture and the gradual changeover from stone to iron tools greatly reinforced the processes of

Right : Market place in Sokoto, northern Nigeria. The leader of a camel caravan approaches the market overseer in the traditional way to report his arrival. Sokoto is one of the many cities of Hausaland, in the fertile valley of the Kebbi river, just on the edge of the arid Sahel. After the great Fulani holy war or 'jihad' of the early nineteenth century, Sokoto became the capital of a huge sultanate which lasted until the British and French conquests at the end of the century. Before the nineteenth century Sokoto was one of the southern termini of the trans-Saharan trade. Gold dust and ingots, and kola nuts, were carried north in camel caravans, in exchange for weapons and above all salt. Salt is mined in the central Sahara, and is vitally important for the diet of West Africans and their animals, living as they do in very hot lands. The salt is often transported in the form of cones, like this one in Sokoto market, which is for passing animals to lick.

Below : Part of a miniature Koran, dating from the late seventeenth or early eighteenth century from Hausa in northern Nigeria. This is essentially a black Koran.

economic, political and social differentiation and led in time to the formation of great kingdoms and empires.

These states and empires of ancient West Africa were scarcely 'popular' in the sense inherited by the European tradition from classical Greece. In almost every case, the impetus for their foundation and growth came from one or two distinctive groups of people, either from outside or inside. First, bands of conquering warriors, often of a different culture and language, forced themselves on an agricultural population—this was certainly the case with Kanem, and possibly with Ghana. Secondly, chiefly clans rose to dominance in encouraging circumstances and managed to accumulate wealth and ultimately political power on a large scale—as was to happen with Mali and Songhay.

Almost without exception, these states were the creation of a single exploitative ruling group, whose power depended on their ability to extort taxes in the form of produce, gold and other trading items, slaves or even the cowrie shell money of the area. Control of trade and traders gave the ruling groups another important source of wealth, while monopoly of religion through the priesthood and through belief in divine kingship allowed them to control, at least in part, the minds and bodies of their subjects. Finally, if all else failed, well-equipped armies could terrorize the populace into submission, so long as their own loyalty was maintained by regular shares in the spoils.

This picture of oppression, exploitation and military thuggery, however, is perhaps unduly gloomy. In spite of many cruelties, West African kingdoms did provide their subjects with some positive advantages. Most important was protection—from the attacks of raiding camelmen, from foreign armies and from slavers. But membership of an empire also gave people a sense of identity, of belonging to a unit much larger and more powerful than the village or kin group. This identity was even spiritual, for divine kings not only inspired fear, awe and obedience, they also were a source of pride and excitement—the heroes of the legends, rituals and dances of many peoples.

Very many of these kingdoms evolved, ranging in size from great empires like Ghana, Mali and Oyo, to hundreds of tiny states such as flourished in Sierra Leone, Guinea, Liberia and the Ivory Coast. Although each state had its own distinctive features there were generally common elements to them all, most notable of which was the 'divine king' or chief. In its most

Below : A rare subject of a woman lying on her back, one of a group of stone carvings from Sierra Leone unearthed by peasants. They may have been put there by an earlier people, and were possibly connected with fertility rites. The woman has tattoos, tribal markings, on her head and body, and her head is supported by a neck rest. The attitude of repose is unique.

developed form the king was held to be a god, not expected to live as ordinary men, but revered and surrounded by rituals. Even lesser kings and chiefs were held to have special contact with the spirit world, as all the rulers of the peoples were seen to be at the point where the spirit world became manifest. The health, fortune and fertility of the society depended absolutely on the king's well-being. Material and spirit worlds were not separated, and so the king's position involved the supernatural sphere of nature gods and ancestral spirits. The kings were central to the cults so necessary to the livelihood of the community and individuals.

The first notable example of a divine kingdom was Ghana. Encouraged by the opportunity for wealth and conquest created by the trans-Saharan trade, little chiefdoms of the Soninke-speaking peoples started upon the road of growth and consolidation to become a powerful state. At first these people lived quite deep into the Sahel, or desert fringe, north of the upper Niger, but in time they were pushed south by the expanding Tuareg. Indeed, the Negro Soninke might have mixed with some of the Caucasoid 'red' Tuareg. Certainly, by the time Muslims first crossed the desert in the middle of the eighth century, they found a thriving Soninke empire known as Ghana or Wagadu with its capital at Kumbi-Saleh, well to the north of the Niger.

Ghana was several centuries old at this time, and was actively involved in the transfer of gold across the Sahara. By the eleventh century it had absorbed certain Islamic influences, while maintaining its pagan kingship, as is shown in a vivid contemporary description:

Above: A so-called Jenné sculpture. These pottery sculptures have come from tumuli, none of which has so far been excavated properly, but some of them have shown that they are fourteenth-century AD and earlier. This one is remarkable for the unique snake depicted on the forehead of the image, which may be a man, a god or a spirit.

'The city of Ghana consists of two towns situated on a plain. One of these towns is inhabited by Muslims. It is large and possesses a dozen mosques, each with imams and salaried reciters of the Koran. There are also jurisconsults and scholars. Around the towns are sweet wells, which they use for drinking and for cultivating gardens. The royal city is six miles away, and the area between the two is covered with habitations. The houses are constructed of stone and acacia wood. The king has a palace of conical shaped houses, surrounded by a fence like a wall. In the king's town, not far from the royal court, is a mosque for the use of Muslims who visit the king on missions. The interpreters of the king are Muslims, as are his treasurer and the majority of his ministers.

    Around the king's town are domed huts and groves where live the sorcerers, the men in charge of their religious cult. In these are also the idols and the tombs of their kings. These groves are guarded, so that no one can enter them or discover their contents. The prisons of the king are there, and if anyone is imprisoned in them, no more is ever heard of him. The religion of the people of Ghana is paganism and the worship of idols.' (al-Bakri, trans N. Levtzion *Ancient Ghana and Mali* London 1973)

The contrast between the two ways of life, the ancient West African and the new Muslim, must have been very striking, but was not unusual, because of the continuing strength of indigenous beliefs.

The origins of divine kingship as it appeared in Ghana are in doubt. It could be that Egyptian ideas of divine kingship, as well as some Egyptian artistic traditions, had spread down the Nile and across the Sudanic plains to West Africa, but this theory is by no means established amongst scholars. There are, nevertheless, many interesting similarities between pharaonic Egypt and the institutions and art of West Africa. The burial customs of Ghana's kings, for instance, were similar to those of the pharaohs (and, incidentally, to other societies):

'When their king dies, they build over the place where his tomb will be an enormous dome of wood. Then they bring him on a bed covered with a few carpets and put him inside the dome. At his side

they place his ornaments, his weapons, and the vessels from which he used to eat and drink, filled with various kinds of food and beverages. They also place there the men who had served his meals. Then they close the door of the dome and cover it with mats and materials, and assemble the people, who heap earth upon it until it becomes like a large mound. Then they dig a ditch around the mound so that it can be reached only at one place. They sacrifice victims for their dead and make offerings of intoxicating drinks.' (*ibid.*)

Other possible origins are the monarchies of South Arabia, Persia and India, but whatever its roots the reverence paid to the Ghanaian kings was absolute. Both nobles and commoners had to obey strict and involved rules of ceremonial submission when entering the god-king's presence. 'When people approach the king of Ghana, they fall on their knees and sprinkle their heads with dust' (al-Bakri). Throughout the kingdoms of the Sudan subjects would prostrate themselves completely before the royal person, remove their clothes, beat their breasts or cover their heads, or the whole body, with dust. The king did not usually address his people directly, but through a spokesman.

The empire of Ghana, however, did not survive long. In 1076 it was overrun, and much of its power destroyed, in an invasion by one of the most powerful of the desert people, the Sanhaja Berbers. They had become fervent Muslims, and launched a conquering crusade north into Morocco and Spain as well as south into Ghana; to the Spaniards they were known as the Almoravids.

In West Africa, the birth and early life of states, often shrouded in mystery, had a great and lasting effect upon later periods of development. Origin myths uniquely affected the person of the king because they were about the beginnings of his family, the ruling dynasty, and inasmuch as the stories were accepted, they provided the means of legitimizing his rule in the eyes of the people. Furthermore, stories of origin—either 'true' or mythical, but certainly believed—were intimately related to the people's religious beliefs and cultural practices as they demonstrated the spiritual— magic or religious—origins of the kings. Indeed, these legends of origin were often the main elements in religion, and therefore in the artistic activities bound up with it. The gods became the first kings—early monarchs who had descended from a black Olympus.

On page 22: A cliff cave in Dogon country. This cave is high up in the Bandiagara escarpment and contains Tellem earth granaries and other objects which indicate that in times of danger the Tellem people retreated to this inaccessible refuge.

On page 23: Terracotta human figure of a type found in burial mounds in the Jenné and Mopti area of Mali. This country, between the Niger and Bani rivers, is flooded for part of each year. It is largely through flooding that the images have come to light over the last two decades.

This is shown particularly in the history of the great empire of Mali, which flourished after the demise of Ghana until well into the fourteenth century. It developed as the families of the *mansa*, the king, of each group of villages, or *kafu*, became identified as the noble clans of the Malinke (another Mande-speaking people, like the Soninke), whose homelands lay across the headwaters of the Niger and Senegal river systems. The eventual kings of Mali belonged to the Keita clan, who ruled a kafu on the Sankarani river, a tributary of the upper Niger. According to Mali traditions (strongly influenced by Islam) the Keita clan was descended from a migrant who came from Mecca. Around 1000 AD, in the reign of Namadi Kani, the Keita chiefdom greatly expanded.

Malian origin myths associate Namadi Kani with the esoteric world of the Malinke hunters, who traditionally organized themselves into secret societies with access to supernatural powers through their close association with the spirits of the bush and the beasts they pursued:

'He was a hunter-king, like the first kings of Mali. It was he who invented the *simbon*, the hunter's whistle; he communicated with the spirits of the forest and the bush. These spirits had no secrets from him, and he was loved by Kondolon and Sane [goddess of the hunters, and her companion]. His followers were so numerous that he formed them into an army which became formidable; he often gathered them together in the bush and taught them the art of hunting. It was he who revealed to hunters the medicinal leaves which heal wounds and cure diseases. Thanks to the strength of his followers he became king of a vast country; with them Namadi Kani conquered the lands which stretch from the Sankarani river to Buré.' (D. T. Niane *Sundiata: An Epic of Old Mali* trans. G. D. Pickett, London 1965)

Above : Tyi-wara dance headdress of the Bambara, Mali. The name means 'farmer with the strength of a wild animal' and the headdress commemorates the mythical half antelope-half man who taught the Bambara their agricultural skills.

Left : A Kaba-blon (shrine) in the small town of Kaba Kangaba on the upper Niger river in Mali. This was the capital of the small Malinke kingdom which grew to become the great empire of Mali in the thirteenth century. This is the shrine building of the Keita clan, whose most illustrious member is the semi-mythical Sundiata, the founder of Mali. This was the only structure not destroyed in the fighting in 1235, and is therefore earlier than that, possibly dating from the third century AD, though repairs are carried out by Keita clansmen every seven years.

The expansion into Buré was very significant—at the time this was the main source of gold in West Africa. By the end of the eleventh century the Keita kafu (called in some documents the kingdom of Kangaba) had achieved a pre-eminence amongst Malinke chiefdoms, but a century later, like most of its neighbours, it was conquered by Sumanguru, king of Susu, one of the successor states of the then defunct empire of Ghana. This was a critical period for the Malinke, who were saved in a war of independence by their hero-king Sundiata, founder of the kingdom of Mali. His story, part myth, part history, is traditionally recounted in a way which shows the full extent of the divine powers associated with kings.

Sundiata was the son of the mansa of Keita by his second wife. The marriage was somewhat mysterious, the bride being given to the mansa by a hunter's society. Sundiata was born a cripple, and as a child had difficulties with his speech. To add to his troubles, he and his mother suffered many slights and insults from the principal wife of the mansa and her son Dankaran Tuma, a tall, handsome and popular young man who was also apparently a fool, but nevertheless succeeded his father as mansa. Sundiata was rescued from his unfortunate predicament by a miracle and the timely intervention of the chief blacksmith, who fitted the young man with some kind of artificial leg.

Once Sundiata was able to stand up and face the world he became a great and terrible warrior and a mighty hunter. Like his ancestor, Namadi Kani, he was awarded the title of *simbon*, granted only to master hunters. Many young men, including some vassal princes, were prepared to follow him, and he became a serious rival to his half-brother, Dankaran Tuma. This so upset Dankaran Tuma's mother, who feared that Sundiata might overthrow her son, that she threatened to kill the upstart. Sundiata's mother then persuaded him to flee with her and his brothers and sisters so as to avoid civil war in Keita. None of the other Malinke kingdoms would give the family refuge, however, for fear of Dankaran Tuma. After much wandering, Sundiata eventually found service at the court of the king of the Soninke state of Mema, well to the north-east of Malinke country, where he became a famed cavalry commander.

While Sundiata was exiled in Mema, Sumanguru, ruler of Susu, over-ran the Malinke kingdoms including Keita. But Sumanguru was so oppressive that Dankaran Tuma and his people rose in revolt, an action which spelled disaster for their kingdom. Sumanguru's soldiers laid waste the land and sacked the capital; many of the royal clan were killed, and Dankaran Tuma fled. Thereafter followed a period of harsh taxation, corrupt government and the seizure of Malinke girls by the arrogant conquerors. Eventually, secret envoys sought out Sundiata to ask him to return and save his people. Provided with horsemen and footsoldiers by the king of Mema, Sundiata advanced into Malinke country where he won a series of battles against Sumanguru and forced him to retreat. The final battle, probably in 1235, took place at Kirina on the banks of the Niger between the lands of the Susu and those of the Malinke.

The legends which surround this decisive battle show how the later inhabitants of the empire of Mali and its successor states invested the founder, Sundiata, with magical powers. The victory is attributed to a confrontation between the powers of witchcraft of the two protagonists. As the armies joined battle, Sumanguru 'uttered a great shout in the face of the warriors of Sundiata, all of whom fled to get behind Sundiata' (H. Delafosse, quoted in B. Davidson *The African Past* London 1964). Whenever Sumanguru thus shouted, he turned into a magical warrior, and 'eight heads would rise above his own head'. Moreover, Sumanguru and his troops had been treated to withstand any wounds made by iron weapons.

Sundiata's magic, however, proved the more potent. One of his lieutenants aimed a spear 'armed with the spur of a white cock' at Sumanguru, shouting: 'This is the spear of him who knows the ancient secrets!' Immediately this struck Sumanguru, he vanished, and was seen no more.

25

Above: A view of Kirina, a Mande village. The trees in the foreground are shea butter trees. The butter—which is not for eating but has a cosmetic use—is produced from the kernels of the 'Bassia parkii' tree, and is known in Mande as 'si'. The drier savannah country to the north, upon which the shea butter tree cannot grow, was regarded by the Malinke inhabitants of the heartlands of ancient Mali as the natural boundary of the mighty empire.

The story tells of a gold bracelet Sumanguru wore on his wrist which fell to the ground. Where it fell a baobab tree grew, carrying the mark of the bracelet. The author of this version of the traditional story, who was writing in 1913, adds: 'Fifty years ago, it is said, the people of Kirina would still show their visitors a baobab tree which they held to be the same one as grew there on the day of Sundiata's famous victory.'

With the defeat of Sumanguru, Sundiata went on to conquer the strongly fortified city of Susu and its neighbouring kingdoms until he had built the empire of Mali, whose name means 'where the king resides'. At the end of his campaigns, a great assembly of Malinke chiefs was held at the site of the ruined capital of the old kingdom of Kangaba. Sundiata rode in triumph in their midst, wearing the costume of a hunter king. One by one the chiefs proclaimed their allegiance, and symbolically surrendered their individual sovereignty to the king.

For his part, Sundiata restored local jurisdiction to each chief, thus maintaining the ancient social and political structure of the Malinke. He assigned special duties and responsibilities, as well as titles and privileges, to his most loyal allies. The ablest among them were to serve him thenceforth as ministers and governors of the provinces of the empire. In many respects, then, the new empire was like the old Kangaba kingdom writ large—it was based firmly on the Malinke lineage system, with the Keita, the clan of the emperor, at the top of the hierarchy.

Sundiata reigned as emperor of Mali until his death in about 1255. Tradition holds that he pushed his conquests to where a tree of the

Sudanic savannah—the shea butter tree—no longer grows, and to this day the Malinke regard this line as their boundary. The old kingdom of Kangaba remains the sacred centre of the Keita clan, where they still meet every seven years to re-enact the building of an ancient religious sanctuary.

After Sundiata the kingdom grew in wealth and splendour, reaching its apogee in the thirteenth century. When in the fourteenth century, the first detailed map of West Africa to be produced in Europe appeared, the work of the Catalan cartographer Abraham Cresques, it showed a regal figure dominating a vast area from his throne; he is named 'Musa Mali, Lord of the Negroes of Guinea'. This was a representation of Mansa Musa the Magnificent, the ruler of Mali, who reigned from 1312 to 1337.

The mainspring of the empire, gold produced both in Malinke country and further south in the forest belt, was now exchanged for salt, cloth, metalware, guns and luxury goods. Mansa Musa had been determined to control all of this highly lucrative commerce, and to bring practically the whole of the western Sudan under his rule. Generals, administrators and tax collectors were sent far and wide to achieve his aims; trading cities such as Timbuktu, Jenné and Gao, famous for their industries and learning, were incorporated into the empire; and Malian soldiers marched deep into the Sahara to capture oases, valuable not only for their salt, but also as staging posts on the caravan routes.

By Mansa Musa's time, Islam had been accepted by many of the ruling classes of the Sudanic countries, and he was one of many rulers who were at least nominally Muslim and shared the consequent obligation to make a pilgrimage to Mecca. Mansa Musa's decision to undertake his pilgrimage in 1324 gave him the opportunity for a fabulous display of wealth, and this famous journey—which took nearly two years to complete—spread the fame of Mali and its ruler far beyond the confines of West Africa.

The emperor travelled with a large retinue which carried the entire state treasury in the form of gold and golden objects which could not be left behind. He stayed a long while in Cairo, *en route* to the Holy City, and his impact there became legendary. In the words of one Egyptian chronicler, 'This man spread upon Cairo the flood of his generosity: there was no person, or officer of the sultanate, who did not receive a sum in gold from him. The people of Cairo earned incalculable sums from him, whether by buying and selling or by gifts. So much gold was current in

Below : Another view of Kirina, one of the three Malinke towns that formed the foundation of Sundiata's empire of Mali. It was here that the famous battle was fought between Sundiata and his rival Sumanguru in 1235. The small structures in this village are grain stores, raised on stones to keep them dry, and to prevent the grain from being eaten by rats and other animals.

Cairo that it ruined the value of money' (al-'Umari, quoted in B. Davidson *The African Past* London 1964).

The same chronicler has left us a splendid description of the court of Mansa Musa, back in Mali:

'The Sultan presides in his palace on a great balcony where he has a huge seat of ebony that is like a throne fit for a large and tall person: on either side it is flanked by elephant tusks turned towards each other. His arms stand near him, being all of gold: sabre, lance, quiver, bow and arrows. He wears wide trousers made of about twenty pieces of cloth of a kind which he alone may wear. Behind him there stand about a score of Turkish or other pages which are bought for him in Cairo: one of them, at his left, holds a silk umbrella surmounted by a dome and a bird of gold: the bird has the figure of a falcon. His officers are seated in a circle about him, in two rows, one to the right and one to the left; beyond them sit the chief commanders of his cavalry. In front of him there is a person who never leaves him and who is his executioner.'

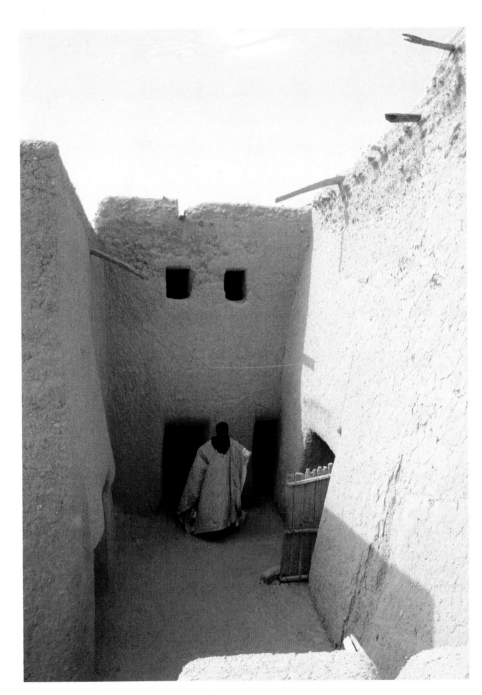

Left : Baobab tree ('Adamsonia digitata') in Malinke country. The baobab is a very ancient and peculiar tree. It has a huge, barrel-like trunk, and when it gets too old and big it becomes top-heavy and falls over. So strange is the baobab that, according to an Arabian legend, the devil plucked it up, thrust its branches into the earth and left its roots in the air. The wood is light and soft and cannot be carved, nor does it last long. The bark, however, is cut and used for rope making, and is thus very important for cliff dwellers and for drawing water out of wells. The fruit of the baobab is large and gourd-like, containing a pleasant, cool-tasting pulp around the seeds. A baobab like this one was for centuries associated with Sundiata's victory.

Right : The Sultan of Agades within a courtyard of his palace. The dried mud walls are built on a wooden framework. The palace of Mansa Musa, Emperor of Mali, would have been larger, but of very similar construction. This palace was first put up in the fourteenth century, and has been constantly repaired.

Islam proved in West Africa to be a very accommodating religion. Providing that the basic tenet of belief in one Supreme God was followed, the older beliefs in a spirit world were untouched. Rulers maintained many, if not most, of their spiritual powers and their status as divine kings. Mansa Musa occupied a position where he was endowed with astonishing powers over his subjects—deriving his powers from pre-Muslim legends of kingship.

As the Mali empire declined in the fifteenth century it was succeeded by Songhay, the last and probably the largest and most powerful of the medieval empires of the western Sudan. The Songhay people lived along the middle reaches of the river Niger, and were composed of three elements —fishermen, farmers and hunters—following complementary livelihoods. The fishermen, called Sorko, were the dominant group, navigating the great river in canoes which not only enabled them to ply their trade, but could also be turned into a fleet of warcraft. The adventurous Sorko were constantly pushing their fishing and fighting expeditions further up the river from their homelands, until they reached a part of the river where they found the herds of hippopotamus and crocodile which they hunted. In their legends the Sorko took on a single mythical character, a fierce river beast with a ring through its nose; they had evidently become identified with their prey.

A riverside town called Kukiya was the capital of this emerging nation of fishermen. Here they came into contact with the fierce Tuareg nomads of the desert to the north, and it is said that the first ruling dynasty of the Songhay was founded by a Berber. An origin myth has it that this stranger was accepted as king after he had killed a 'fish dragon' (a hippopotamus or a crocodile); the fish dragon was then worshipped by the Songhay, who had to obey its stern commands. West African mythology shows many instances of dragons becoming a new chief or king, and such myths appear to represent a successful challenge by a conquering group to the authority of the long-established 'priests of the land' and the assumption of their spiritual power.

Through their contact with the Berbers, the Songhay became involved in the lucrative trans-Saharan trade and, in the eighth century AD, moved their main city up the Niger to Gao which became the administrative capital of Songhay, while Kukiya remained the religious centre. This steady advance eventually brought them face to face with the power of Mali, which conquered most of the Songhay country, including Gao. Just as Sundiata's Malinke had rebelled against their masters so did the Songhay, and the struggle for their independence brought about a new ruling dynasty, called the Sonni. The little river kingdom slowly extended its territory as the Mali empire declined.

The man who finally turned the kingdom of canoeists into a vast empire was Sonni Ali the Great, another legendary West African hero. Coming to the throne at the death of his father in 1464 Sonni Ali was later known in much of West Africa as Ali Ber, Ali the Great. In Songhay itself, however, he was simply called 'the Shi', a corruption of the title Sonni. He was only nominally a Muslim; indeed, he earned the hatred of Islamic historians, both in his own time and later. These writers no doubt exaggerated his temperamental character, but he was certainly responsible for many acts of great brutality. While insulting him as an impious Muslim, however, the chroniclers could not entirely suppress pride in his achievements.

Unlike Sundiata, Sonni Ali had a privileged and even a pampered upbringing, but one in which magic played a large part; it was widely held that the art of magic was suckled with the mother's milk. In the words of one Muslim chronicler: 'His mother originated from the country of Sokoto. This is an infidel nation, which worships wooden and stone idols. Should some good or evil happen, it is the idols which have been favourable or unfavourable. War is not made unless they have given their judgement. The false gods, to serve them and worship them, have priests directed by diviners and witch doctors who also give consultations. Sonni Ali spent all

Left : Sunrise, with canoes on the river Bani at Mopti, Mali. This is in Mande country, upstream from Songhay and Timbuktu. The Bani river is a tributary of the Niger, the great artery of West Africa. Its headwater streams rise in the Futa Jallon mountains of Guinea, about 300 km (less than 200 miles) from the Atlantic, but the huge river—the third largest in Africa after the Nile and the Congo—flows 4,200 km (about 2,600 miles) north-east and then south-east before it reaches the Atlantic in the Bight of Benin. Its name might come from the Latin 'niger', 'black', but it is more likely to derive from the Berber/Tuareg word 'n'eghiren', 'stream'. The Mande people call it Joliba, 'the great big river'. Between Ségou and Timbuktu there is an immense, fertile 'inland delta' the size of England and Wales. The northernmost part of the great Niger bend, from Timbuktu to Bourem, actually flows through the Sahara Desert. Between Yelwa and Jebba in Nigeria there is a series of rapids, impassable even by canoe. These rapids effectively cut off the middle from the lower section of the Niger, and have ensured that these sections have played separate roles in the history of West Africa.

31

Above: A robe, worn by men, from Hausa, northern Nigeria. It is of dyed cotton—blue with indigo—and embroidered with silk thread. Such work reveals strong traces of Islamic influence.

his youth among these men and his mind received the imprint of their idolatry and of their customs.' Through his father, Sonni Ali inherited the powers of the 'witch doctor kings' of Kukiya, the descendants of the 'dragon killer'. He was in contact with sorceresses whose practices, we are told, were a hotch-potch of black African, Christian, Berber and Oriental occultism. To add to his supernatural powers, the young prince was initiated by his own father, a custom for high-ranking fathers still observed by the Songhay. At the initiation ceremony he received the secret word which made gods and spirits of every kind his submissive servants. When he came to the throne, Sonni Ali was held to be the most powerful magician the region had ever known, and the spiritual prestige of his descendants today is but a pale reflection of the magician-king's renown.

To attribute the extraordinary military and organizational success of Sonni Ali to supernatural powers may seem strange now, but his contemporaries never doubted that magic was his strength. Year after year, during a twenty-seven-year reign, he led his armies from one end of the Sudanic Niger region to the other and never, it seems, suffered a major setback. 'The tyrant, the profligate, the accursed one, the oppressor, the Shi Ali, was always victorious; when he was present, none of his armies was defeated,' wrote a shocked Muslim. Songhay traditions relate that Sonni Ali made his soldiers and his horses take magic charms, by means of which they could fly in the sky, make themselves invisible or change into serpents. He himself turned into a vulture, and transformed his wonder horse, Zinzinbadio, into another. It is thus that he is represented on the little silver ring of one of his descendants.

The armies of Sonni Ali incorporated more and more peoples into the empire, many of which were the sworn enemies of Songhay, forcibly brought under its sway. When suitably pacified or rewarded, however, they often became its most valiant soldiers. Such was the case with the Tuareg, the black-veiled camelmen of the desert, and with the Dogon cliff people in the mountains south of the Niger bend, both of whom had a reputation for bravery. Present-day Songhay have retained traditions of the martial feats of the Dogon 'peoples of the mountains'. But the most remarkable arm of Songhay military establishment was the fleet of war canoes on the Niger, manned by Sorko fishermen, who as we have seen were the earliest component of Songhay power.

The naval flotilla ensured that the Niger, the main artery of the empire, remained open for communications and for the transport of commerce and war materials. Sonni Ali used the fleet to push his conquests westwards into the old Mali country, and during the seven-year siege of Jenné, the great walled city was blockaded by 400 canoes. So aware was the emperor of the importance of river power that when he planned to attack a city 320 kilometres (200 miles) from the Niger he began building a canal, clearing away sand to allow the river to flow up one of its old courses.

Sonni Ali died in mysterious circumstances. Returning from a campaign in November 1492 he was drowned 'in a torrent-like river'—at a time of year when nearly all the water courses would have been dry. His soldiers buried him in an unmarked grave. The empire that owed so much to the iron will of Sonni Ali lasted a further 100 years, until it was overthrown in 1591 by a Moroccan army. But Sonni Ali is remembered in mythology not only as a powerful king and magician, but also as a god: he has become the great and dangerous Za, the father of the spirit of the water.

While Ghana, Mali and Songhay rose and fell, another ancient kingdom flourished far to the east. Travellers from Tunisia passed south through the desert via the Fezzan oases, along a route to Kawar, with its salt-producing oasis of Bilma, and finally to Lake Chad. Just north of the lake was the kingdom of Kanem, which had been founded early in the Christian era by waves of invading Zhagawa and Magumi: unlike the Tuareg invaders of the western Sudan, these camelmen were Negroes.

The conquerers established a dynasty of kings called *mais* which would continue to rule in unbroken succession until the nineteenth century—one

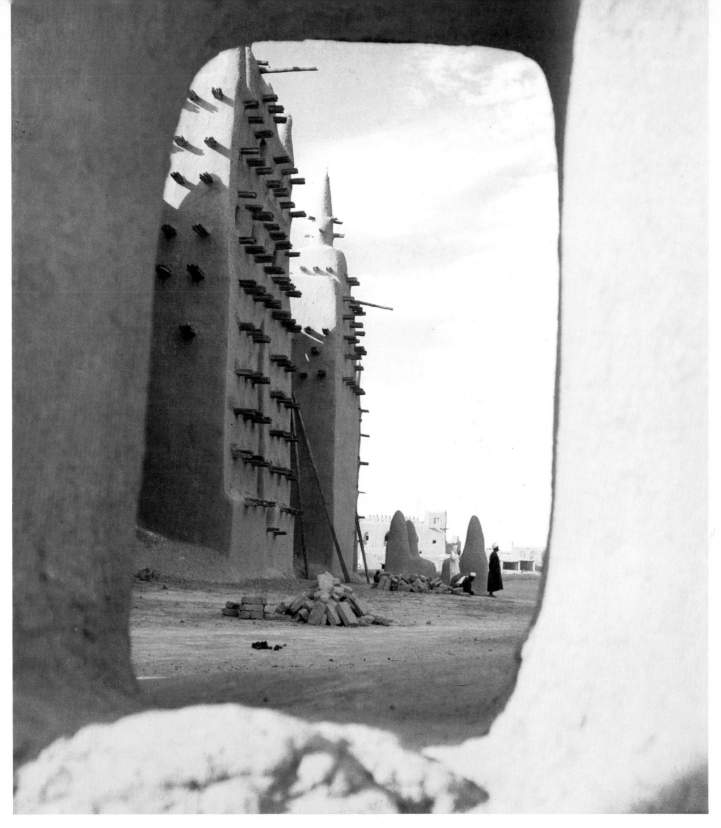

of the longest lines of kings in history. The mais were considered by their subjects to be gods dwelling amongst them. One tenth-century indignant Muslim wrote:

'They exalt and worship him instead of God. They imagine that he does not eat, for his food is introduced into his compound secretly, no-one knowing whence it is brought. Should one of his subjects happen to meet the camel carrying his provisions, he is killed instantly on the spot . . . He has absolute power over his subjects and takes what he will of their belongings. Their religion is the worship of kings, for they believe that it is they who bring life and death and sickness and health.' (Yaqut, *Kitab mu'jam al-buldan*, ed. F. Wüstenfeld, Leipzig 1886)

Above: The great mosque of Jenné. There is very little stone for building purposes in West Africa, and in the Sudanic belt very large buildings such as this were constructed of dried mud on a wooden framework—the ends of the framework jutting out of the walls.

33

The taboo on witnessing the king eating and drinking, and performing other natural functions, was very common in West Africa. In early Songhay: 'When the king sits down to eat a drum is beaten and no one is allowed to travel about the town until the king finishes his repast.' In Mali the king was not allowed to be seen eating, even by his wives who served the food. When Mansa Musa visited Cairo, it was recorded that no one was allowed to sneeze in the royal presence, and when the king himself sneezed those present beat their breasts with their hands. Centuries later, a European anthropologist described how in Junkun, a kingdom in Nigeria, all those present slapped their thighs respectfully when the ruler sneezed.

The kingdom of Kanem was aggressively militaristic. The cavalry raided deep amongst the Negro peoples to the south to capture slaves, who were put to work in the kingdom or exported across the Sahara to Muslim North Africa. By the end of the eleventh century, the ruler of Kanem had himself embraced Islam, one of the first kings of Black Africa to do so. But the main thrust of Kanem was expansion southwards, and as the mais continued to be harassed by incursions of desert warriors, the capital shifted by the fifteenth century from north-east of Lake Chad to Bornu, to the south-west. The mixture of newcomers from old Kanem and the local people of Bornu produced the Kanuri people, who were some of the most highly Islamicized in West Africa.

Islam, however, never fully supplanted the ancient religions in the areas where it took root. It penetrated far into the northern areas of West Africa, but, with one or two exceptions, scarcely at all into the less centralized states of the south. But even in the north the majority of the peoples maintained their allegiance to their traditional religions, and many rulers, like Sonni Ali, professed Islam but still enjoyed the status of divine king. Nevertheless, the effect of Islam on many societies was profound and long-standing. Through a process of reciprocal change, this universal religion moulded African life and at the same time was moulded by Africans in every element of religious experience—in myth, in cult and in fellowship. Ultimately Islam became almost an indigenous religion, a natural part of the West African scene.

When it first appeared in the northern Sudanic regions, from the ninth century onwards, Islam was adopted by some of the ambitious rulers of the great medieval states as an instrument of policy—generally directed at improving relations with the powers in North Africa and the Middle East, but also as an important innovation in domestic politics. Some did not actually convert to the new religion, but permitted Muslim merchants, artisans, clerics and teachers to live at their courts—often in a separate quarter of the town. Such was the case in the kingdom of Ghana. But the rulers of Kanem-Bornu, of Mali, of Songhay and of the Hausa states did convert. Many of their subjects also became Muslims, but some rulers would not allow this. The new faith was a powerful politico-religious instrument, but might prove dangerous if unleashed indiscriminately.

Sonni Ali, for all his own sound knowledge of Islam, both feared and respected the power of Islamic scholars. He eliminated any whose 'magical-religious' powers might prove equal or superior to his own, and sought to prevent his priests and magicians, and members of his court from acquiring knowledge of Islam. For all his ruthlessness, Sonni Ali was shrewd enough to see that survival depended on maintaining a balance between traditional Songhay religion and Islam.

The magical powers associated with Islam were something proselytizing Muslims did not fail to exploit. Despite their adherence to traditional religious practices, the majority of West Africans viewed Islamic rituals with considerable awe. Religious specialists such as clerics and diviners were in great demand for the services they could render such as sand-divining, praying, and supplying charms and amulets, which usually contained extracts from the Koran written on small pieces of paper or in the sand. The Nafana people of modern west Ghana, for example, remained

Above: Part of a woman's dress of woven cloth from the Bambara people of Mali. The brown and red colours are natural dyes. The design is not a collection of arbitrary or 'artistic' patterns. It is part of the symbolic or 'idea' language of the Bambara. The lizard or tortoise representation is shared with many other West African peoples, and has a deep religious significance.

Left : A detail of a horse harness made of leather, hammered brass and copper from Bornu, northern Nigeria. The ancient empire of Bornu, the largest and longest surviving of the central Sudan, was a militarist state which relied upon heavily armoured Kanuri cavalry to maintain its sway over neighbouring peoples.

Above: Examples of wooden carved parchment boards, made in Nupe, Nigeria, which were used as protective covering for precious parchment documents, such as the Koran. They were known as 'panko' book covers.

staunchly pagan, while utilizing the power of Islam for additional protection. They attached both Muslim amulets and non-Muslim fetishes to royal chairs and stools. Muslim prayers and medicine were also used, in case Nafana priests and medicine-men failed.

Although some Muslim West African rulers became renowned for the strength and purity of their faith, in time the majority became comparatively lax—at least in the estimation of the fiery reformers of Islam. Right from the beginning Islam in West Africa had proved extremely flexible, except perhaps in the basic tenet of the faith, 'there is but one God, Allah, and Muhammad is his prophet'. It could co-exist with a host of traditional West African religious beliefs and customs. The ritual surrounding royalty in West Africa was retained, and beliefs in ancestors, magic and spirits, good or bad, were acceptable to all but the purists.

Royal patronage was very important to the Muslims, who were minority communities in most West African societies. But, exceptionally for a state-supported religion, there was rarely a professional priestly class of upholders of Islam. There were 'official' judges and learned men, who interpreted and maintained the legal and theological standards of the faith, and there were officials of the mosques, but most performed these functions part-time.

Away from the political orbits of the Sudanic kingdoms the main disseminators of Islam were 'non-professionals', itinerant merchants, tradesmen and artisans. In the western part of West Africa the Mande-speaking Dyula traders were largely responsible for the spread of Islam. Each of their many settlements became a focal point of the Muslim faith. The Dyula did not necessarily propagate their religion actively, but many non-Muslims were attracted to them as powerful sources of magic and spiritual influence.

Occasionally, from among the most thoroughly Muslimized peoples— like the Mande-speakers, the Fulani and the Tuareg (see chapter 4)—there emerged individuals of great religious power. These were the holy men or saints of Islam. Their renown as men ardent in the faith and immaculate in their morals, as well as their fame as healers and bringers of good fortune, attracted large followings. These Muslim saints often founded or joined religious orders, and it was the leaders of these orders who proclaimed the *jihads* (holy wars) in the eighteenth and nineteenth centuries.

The most famous and erudite of the reformers was the Fulani Uthman dan Fodio, whose jihad led to the establishment of a vast, united Muslim caliphate over the Hausa states. Although the Hausa rulers had already professed Islam, Uthman denounced them for their pagan practices: 'They practise polytheistic rituals and turn people away from the path of God and raise the flag of worldly kingdom above the banner of Islam. All this is unbelief according to the consensus of opinion. The government of a country is the government of its king without question. If the king is a Muslim, his land is Muslim; if he is an Unbeliever, his land is a land of Unbelievers.'

Yet the significance of Islam was not just religious or political. Centuries earlier, the same zeal that drove Uthman dan Fodio east across the savannah had sent jihads west along the Mediterranean shores. In their wake had come not only merchants but clerics and teachers, crossing the desert to an unknown land. Timbuktu and Jenné became centres of learning for scholars from all over North Africa and the Sudan. And one of the great contributions these Muslim clerics made was to record West African history, particularly giving the outside world a picture of these kingdoms of the northern Sudan.

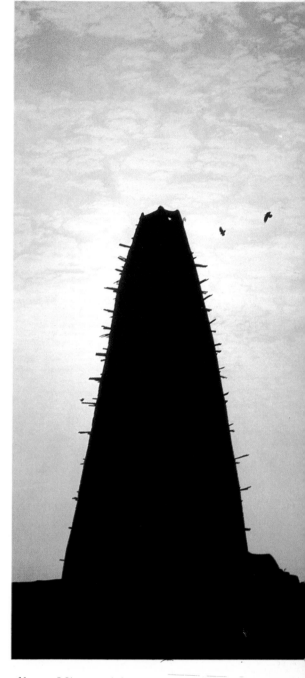

Above: Minaret of the mosque of Agades, which was originally built in the fourteenth century. Islam—a universal religion—was extremely flexible in everything but its fundamental tenets, and could adapt to local circumstances; in this case, to the arid environment of the Sahara.

Left: Palace of the Emir of Argungu, on the Kebbi river, a tributary of the Niger, in Northern Nigeria. Argungu was one of many emirates established by the Fulani 'jihad' of Uthman dan Fodio within the great sultanate of Sokoto. The interior of this palace shows the cool and harmonious effects that can be achieved by traditional construction materials and methods.

The Kingdoms
of the South

The difficulty the British experienced in dealing with the King
was due to the fact that he was himself a big ju-ju, in which
the natives had unbounded confidence. They believed he
would never be captured, and that if the British did succeed in
arriving at the city, he would turn into a bird or some animal
and so escape.

(H. Ling Roth *Great Benin – Its Customs, Art and Horrors*
London 1903)

The early societies inhabiting the belt of dense rain forest which runs across
the southern fringe of West Africa and the wooded savannah further north
remained virtually undisturbed long after the creation of populous kingdoms and empires in the northern Sudanese zone. Gradually, however,
the use of iron tools enabled them to clear more ground and produce better
harvests, which led to a fairly rapid expansion of population, and trade
with the north grew increasingly important to the local economies. The
first of the powerful southern states had certainly been founded by the
early fifteenth century, and over the next 300 years several dynamic
civilizations would emerge. In fact, of the six or more large groups of
peoples who lived in the eastern wooded belt—from modern Ghana to
Nigeria—only the Ibo did not develop a form of organization above the
level of local village headmen and elders. They did, however, have a single
religious authority, an oracle to whom all inter-tribal disputes were
brought. It seems probable that this type of 'low level' political activity,
with a unifying religious bond, was common to most of the southern groups
—and indeed to the majority of West African peoples—until they were
seriously disturbed by outside influences such as migrant groups coming
amongst them, military adventurers, or the lures of profitable trade beyond
the confines of village markets. The arrival of Europeans, outflanking the
Muslim trade monopoly by sailing round the West African coast, would
eventually transform all the societies of the south.

One of the most culturally brilliant of these states, and also the most
politically and militarily formidable, was the Yoruba kingdom of Oyo,
situated to the north and west of the tropical rain forest. It was already a
great kingdom in the fifteenth century, when the Portuguese arrived off
the coast of West Africa, but it did not reach its zenith until the eighteenth.
We have to rely mainly on legends—traditional history—to throw light
upon the origins of Oyo and its early history. For although the hero chiefs
who appear in the traditions are unlikely to have been historical figures,
there is a sense in which they are vibrant and alive; they became members
of the Yoruba pantheon, god-men who were believed to have directly
influenced the course of history.

39

There are two main Yoruba origin myths, one suggesting that the Yoruba were the original inhabitants of the core region around the religious centre of Ife, the other that the ancestors of the Yoruba ruling classes came from afar. The first, a creation myth, tells that in the beginning the world was a 'watery waste'. God ordered his son, Oduduwa, to climb down from the heavens on a chain, and to carry with him a handful of earth, a cockerel and a palm nut. Once at the foot of the chain, Oduduwa scattered the earth on the face of the water and formed, at Ife, the first land. The cockerel then scratched a hole in the earth, into which Oduduwa planted the palm nut. From the nut grew an immense tree with sixteen branches, and each branch became a ruling family of Yoruba state. This great chain of Oduduwa is still preserved at Ife among the most sacred relics of the Yoruba people.

The other story depicts Oduduwa as the son of a mighty king of the east. He was forced to leave his homeland, and wandered with his followers for many years. Eventually they were made welcome by the forest folk of West Africa, settled amongst them, and founded the city of Ife. Oduduwa had seven sons who left the palace at Ife, and set up kingdoms of their own—the seven states which, with Ife itself, comprised historical Yorubaland. Oyo and Benin were included in these seven.

According to the legends, Oranyan, the youngest son of Oduduwa, was abandoned by his brothers during a military expedition against the people who lived to the north of Yoruba country. A local chief had compassion on him, and presented him with a great snake with a magic charm twined round its neck, telling Oranyan to follow the snake for seven days until it stopped and disappeared into the ground. He duly followed the snake through the bush, and founded the city of Oyo on the spot where it disappeared.

Oranyan had a son called Sango who succeeded him as *alafin*, or king, of Oyo. He had a reputation for being a mighty warrior and a powerful magician, who made many conquests. He breathed fire and smoke, and boasted of being able to control thunder and lightning, but one day he tried to put this boast to the test, with dire consequences. When he called

On page 38 : The sword ceremony of Benin Chief Okonghae Ogiamwen, performed in the kingship shrine in the courtyard of the palace. Since the building had to be defended, it has no windows, and indeed all the important buildings in Benin were destroyed during a British punitive expedition except the house of the Chief Ogiamwen. This authentic ceremony, which consists of swirling and rotating the 'eben' or ceremonial sword-sceptre, is performed during coronation celebrations of the obas and the all-important annual Benin festival of 'igue'. The ceremonial dress, known as 'ehaengbehia', is reserved for the oba or ogiamwen, and the ceremonial crown is called 'ede'.

Left: The Portuguese reached the coast of the kingdom of Benin at the end of the fifteenth century, and soon made a visual impact on Benin art. This sixteenth-century bronze plaque of two Portuguese men, possibly seamen in their shoregoing outfits, has some touches of humour in the marked differences in height and the man on the left stroking his beard.

Right: A broken Benin bronze of about 1600, depicting a warrior chief with an assortment of weapons and two attendant soldiers who carry shields and more weapons. The fact that the chief's sword and headdress are the same as those shown on p. 38 is an indication of how old the ceremonial regalia must be. His typical coral-bead necklace signifies high rank, and the jaguar-teeth necklace beneath it, with its magico-protective purpose, is the mark of the hunter. In the background are two small musicians, one blowing a horn and the other banging clappers.

the lightning down to earth, it set fire to his palace and destroyed his entire family. The over-proud alafin was humbled. Filled with remorse, and harried by the people of Oyo, he fled into the forest and hanged himself. That was not the end of Sango, however; the Yoruba forgave him his arrogance, or perhaps in retrospect admired him for it, and made him their god of thunder and war, bestowing on him the form of a ram. So powerful was the god Sango that, when later the Yoruba states quarrelled bitterly among themselves, to exhibit his emblems was often sufficient to bring about peace.

Like the Ibo, their neighbours to the east of the Niger, the Yoruba relied on forest farming for their livelihood, but their political life was based on the city, and not the village. In many respects the Yoruba shared Ibo skills in iron-smelting, brasswork, cotton-weaving and other valuable handicrafts, but it was their cities that comprised their special contribution to West African civilization. They had large populations, and were usually surrounded by a defensive wall; indeed, the wall around old Oyo, the capital of the Oyo empire, was as much as 40 kilometres (25 miles) round, and at least 6 metres (20 feet) high.

Old Oyo was situated in the northern marches of Yorubaland, in open

woodland country. It was ideally sited for cavalry warfare—in which its inhabitants came to excel—and for control over the rich trade routes leading into Hausaland and the Sudanic regions. Oyo expanded until it came to dominate all the other Yoruba states, which formed subordinate units in the new empire. The *obas*, or rulers of these states, owed allegiance to the alafin. As the earliest Yoruba state, however, Ife remained the religious heart of the country—it was a sanctuary, safe from any attack by the Yoruba themselves, and the royal treasure and sacred emblems of Oranyan were protected there.

Much of the wealth and power of Oyo was derived from participation in the trans-Atlantic slave trade. Oyo controlled the trading states along the coast from Lagos to the frontier of modern Ghana, and was able for a long time to keep a tight rein on the developing kingdom of Dahomey, which was some distance inland from the coast. But nemesis awaited the empire. Early in the nineteenth century it collapsed under the dual forces of Dahomey's new-style totalitarian state and the war bands of the fiercely Muslim Fulani. For the remainder of that century Yorubaland was plagued by one civil war after another, until it was finally taken over by the British in the 1890s.

Like the Sudanic kings, the alafins of Oyo were believed to be appointed by the gods. To each new alafin was revealed the secrets of the sacred cults and all the mysteries of kingship. Thereafter he became *Ejeki Orisa*, no longer human but companion of the immortal. He alone could appoint cult priests and government officials, and this patronage, both religious and secular, gave him supreme control of all the instruments of state.

Yet the Oyo also developed an extraordinary system of checks and balances, which in practice greatly reduced the power of the alafin and his entourage. Power-hungry officials of the alafin cannot have been encouraged by the knowledge that at the alafin's death they too were to die, along with the monarch's retinue. Even the king's eldest son was to kill himself—a tradition which must have dampened any desire for intrigues around an heir-apparent. This general suicidal slaughter ensured that the newly appointed king began his reign with only spiritual traditions and the Council of State, a body of elders who were independent of the alafin, to influence him.

The new alafin was selected by the seven members of this Council, headed by a chief minister, after painstaking consultation with the oracle at Ife to determine which of the candidates from among the royal family was the favourite of the gods. Even in power he was seldom able to ignore the wishes of either the Council of State or the chief minister, and he also had to be wary of the Ogboni, the secret society dedicated to the cult of the earth and made up of highly influential freemen. The Ogboni tried any judicial case involving the spilling of blood, as such a crime profaned Mother Earth, and it was so powerful that it could dictate terms to all but the most assertive alafins.

Moreover, since the alafin was so intimately involved with the religious rituals of his state, he was effectively cut off from contact with ordinary people and from politics. The chief minister, of course, was immersed in them. If both the Council of State and the Ogboni society decided to reject the alafin, their members could instruct the chief minister to take the necessary action. He presented the alafin with either an empty calabash or a dish of parrot's eggs, uttering these dreadful words: 'The gods reject you, the people reject you, the earth rejects you.' The miserable alafin then had to commit suicide by taking poison.

At the collapse of the Oyo empire the reigning alafin, Awole, was blamed for the catastrophe and received this terrible rejection from the chief minister. Awole bade his family and friends farewell, and made the necessary arrangements for the ceremonial suicide. Before he drank the poison, however, he fired arrows in every direction, and proclaimed a bitter curse: 'My curse be on you for your disloyalty and your disobedience, so let your children disobey you. If you send them on an errand, let them never return to bring you word again. To all the points I shoot my arrows will you be carried off as slaves. My curse will carry to the sea and beyond the seas, slaves will rule over you, and you their masters will become slaves. Broken calabash can be mended but not a broken dish; so let my words be irrevocable.'

Awole's famous curse has had a ring of prophecy. For much of the nineteenth and twentieth centuries, up to the Nigerian Civil War of 1967 to 1970, the Yoruba experienced several misfortunes. But they have not forgotten their legends.

The Yoruba legends also recount the origins of the obas of Benin, which lay to the south of Oyo and just to the west of the vast Niger delta, in an area of immensely thick tropical rain forest. Unlike almost every other West African empire, Benin was wholly a forest state. Its traditions recount a line of kings stretching back long before contact with the Oyo, but it seems that at that early time Benin was just a tiny domain on one of the many rivers lost in the sprawling jungle. The petty rulers fell out with their people, the Edo, who wanted, so we are told, a republican form of government—perhaps modelled on the neighbouring Ibo. During these disputes, an envoy was sent to Oduduwa, the ruler of Ife, asking him to send one of his sons to be king of Benin.

Oduduwa, however, not knowing whether he could trust the Edo, set a test for them. He sent seven lice to the chiefs of Benin with instructions to look after them and return them at the end of three years. The Edo passed their test; Oduduwa was surprised to see his lice not only safe and sound but even increased in size. 'The people', he said, 'who can take care of such minute pests as lice can surely take care of my son.'

Oduduwa died soon afterwards, but his youngest son, the same Oranyan who was later to become the founder of Oyo, duly set out for Benin accompanied by a witch doctor and a priest as a protection against the dangers on the way. When Oranyan reached Benin, although many of the old ruling family did not want him there, the people welcomed him and soon proclaimed him as their oba. He took up residence in a palace built especially for him which still survives as a coronation shrine. Although he married and had a son, Oranyan did not take to Benin and its inhabitants. Eventually, he summoned a meeting of the people and renounced the

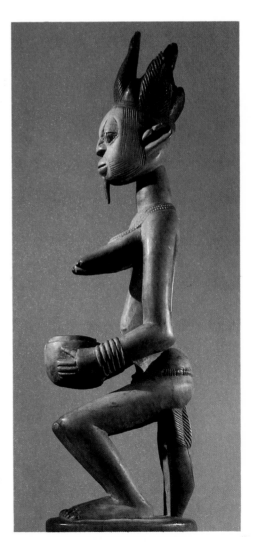

Below: Wooden figure from a shrine at the village of Ilobu, near Oshogbo, Yorubaland. The ornate hair style and the lip plug are ancient features of this kind of statue, but are now obsolete. The fecundity of the woman is stressed; she is holding a bowl for offerings to the god or spirits of the shrine.

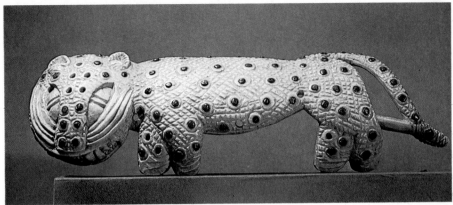

obaship, saying that the country was a land of vexation, and that only a child born, trained and educated in its arts and mysteries could reign over the people. His son therefore became oba, and Oranyan returned to Ife, where began the sequence of events that led him to Oyo. The ties between Benin and Ife held firm, however, and the remains of every third oba of Benin were taken to the shrine at Ife.

Benin was already a very powerful state when the Portuguese arrived along the coast in 1486. The empire's most famous oba, Ewuare the Great, ruled from about 1440 to 1473. His predecessor, who had banished Ewuare, was murdered and Ewuare was recalled. His name meant 'the trouble has ceased', but before he accepted the obaship, he took a terrible revenge for his banishment, burning down much of the city in a fire lasting two days and nights. In spite of his vengeance, Ewuare is remembered as a great magician, physician, traveller and warrior. During his reign he made good, wide roads in Benin and the town grew to importance and became a city. He made powerful charms and had them buried at each of the nine gateways to nullify any evil charms which might be brought by people from other countries to injure his subjects. He greatly encouraged ivory- and wood-carving in Benin, and was himself the inventor of a wind instrument like a fife. His statesmanship earned for him the title Ewuare Ogidigan—Ewuare the Great.

Ewuare made the position of oba of Benin much more powerful in practice than that of the alafin of Oyo. The oba, and not a council of state or any secret society, was in complete control. The king, in fact, became the principle object of adoration in his dominions—not only the gods' vice-regent upon earth, but a god himself, whose subjects both obeyed and adored him as such. The oba's subjects believed that he required neither food nor sleep, and that when he died, he was destined to reappear on earth at the end of a fixed period.

A seventeenth-century Dutch writer described the courts of the oba:

'No man is allowed to wear any dress at all at court before he has been clothed by the king; nor let his hair grow before this has been done. There are men at the king's court, twenty and twenty-four years old, who, without any semblance of shame go about naked, only wearing a chain of corals or jasper round their necks. But when the king gives them clothes, he usually presents them at the same time with a wife, thus making them from boys into men. After this time they always wear clothes and let their hair grow without being obliged to shave it off with a knife any more.' (William Bosman *A New and Accurate Description of the Coast of Guinea* London 1705)

In the days before the trans-Atlantic slave trade, the lives of the inhabitants of Benin City and the surrounding countryside reflected the security provided by such a mighty ruler. The obas, however powerful, did not terrorize either their own subjects or their neighbours: indeed, Benin developed a vigorous legal system, with strong traditions of justice.

45

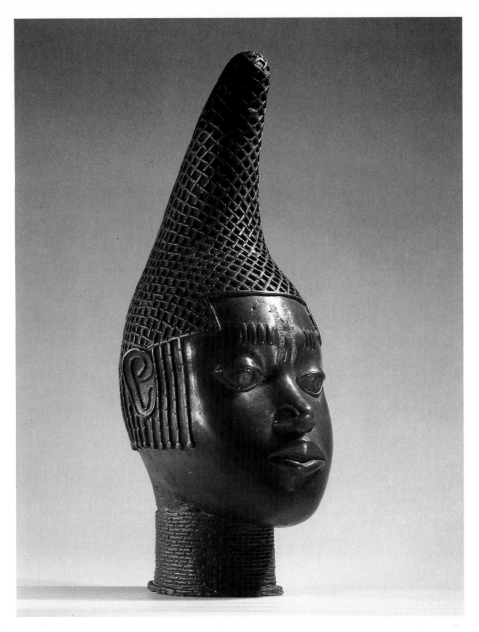

One Dutch observer remarked that 'the king is considered just and equitable, as desiring continuously his officers to administer justice exactly, and to discharge their duties conscientiously. He seldom passes one day without holding a cabinet council with his chief ministers, for dispatching of the many affairs brought before him.' Thus the obas of ancient Benin successfully combined the roles of god, despot and approachable father of their people.

The splendour of the city, the impressiveness of its culture, the attractiveness of its rituals and the prestige and power of the oba were in many respects more important than military expeditions in cementing the alliances between the oba and the smaller states, towns and villages which became the clients of Benin. In the fifteenth century, the authority and influence of the oba, through these client states, reached an area roughly twice the size of England and Wales. The oba generally sent out members of the royal family as provincial governors, but the power and prestige of Benin also drew professionals in many fields to live in the capital—not only sculptors and other artists, but also experts in medicine, diviners and men of religion. Recruitment into the palace occupations, such as legal, military and religious administration, was thrown open to people from all over the empire, thus ensuring the participation of talented individuals in the government.

Benin remained a splendid city, the worthy capital of a wealthy empire,

for several centuries. But the ravages of the slave trade, and conflicts with rival states, ushered in a long period of decline during the eighteenth century. Benin stagnated while neighbours prospered, and the once dynamic empire turned in upon itself, becoming introspective and self-destructive. The worst symptom was a great increase in human sacrifice. The killing of servants and followers was a common West African practice on the death of a person of importance and substance, but in normal times and conditions this human sacrifice was on a very small scale, and victims were never terrorized. As Benin became more and more isolated and threatened, the number of human sacrifices increased, until by the end of the nineteenth century the practice was on an immense scale. The greater the external threat, the more the gods and ancestors had to be propitiated. There is no reason to doubt that the victims of these mass slaughters, other than slaves or captives, went willingly to their deaths, believing that death was necessary for the continued independence of their homeland. But in 1897 the oba was captured by the British and sent into exile, ending a dynasty and a civilization that had expressed itself with more artistic skill and more terrifying devotions than almost any other West African culture.

The Fon people of Dahomey also created a remarkable, centralized state. They lived inland from the shores which became notorious as the Slave Coast, and, finding themselves continually raided by slavers, in about 1680 they organized a strong, initially defensive unit: the Kingdom of Dahomey. Tradition has it that the founder was the son of a union between a leopard and a human princess, and that his fierce and valiant spirit derived from his leopardine parentage. The first kings of historical times won the support of the people by peaceful means, with 'lavish hospitality and open-handed generosity', but they also stressed their religious position as the 'lords of the land' who initiated annual ceremonies of sacrifice to propitiate the gods.

This quiet form of monarchy continued until Agaja came to the throne in 1708. A proud, charismatic leader, he was both dignified and courteous, with a quick sense of humour and great generosity to his friends. He had a fine grasp of the motivation of men, be they African or European. But it was his military and statesmanlike qualities that really allowed him to stamp his mark on history. He himself was totally resolute and he had the rare ability to restore the morale of his men in the aftermath of defeat. In a reign lasting twenty-four years, he imposed his will with such effect that he changed the course of his kingdom's politics beyond all expectation.

In Agaja's Dahomey all property in the state belonged to the king, who used his monopoly of wealth and trade to build up a highly efficient and loyal army. Both military and civil officials were the king's men; they owed their office to Agaja, and not to an inherited position. Dahomey was encompassed by enemies, with Oyo on one side, Asante on the other, and the slaving states on the coast. This situation of almost continuous emergency instilled a unity and a sense of dynamism so intense that the people of Dahomey expressed their loyalty in a telling simile. They saw the life of the nation as a pot with many holes. Only if all citizens kept their fingers firmly over the holes could the life-giving force, the royal power, be prevented from draining away. Unusually for West Africa, women too were called into the service of the state—in particular the famous 'Amazon' regiments of women soldiers in the royal army.

To pursue his aim of creating a powerful Dahomey, Agaja first challenged the ruler of a coastal state which controlled the trade of the area. Since this ruler was the senior member of the Aja ruling class, of which the Fon of Dahomey were merely one section, Agaja's conflict with him was openly revolutionary, flying in the face of all accepted political and religious institutions. Yet although he was undoubtedly one of the most radical kings ever to rule in West Africa, forcefully discarding institutions and people in his way, Agaja was always careful to build on the semi-divine status of Dahomey kingship which had been created by his predecessors.

While Dahomey was militarily engaged with the coastal slaving states

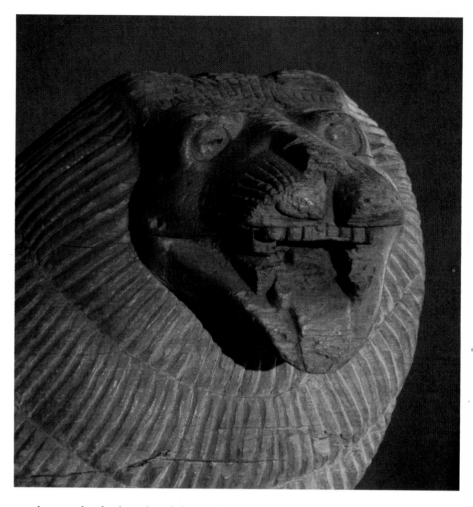

to the south, during the eighteenth century, the Fon remained tributaries to their neighbour, the mighty Oyo empire. In the nineteenth century, however, Dahomey helped to overthrow Oyo, and ravaged Yorubaland. Dahomey's military power suffered no serious check until the end of the century, when the French, in a hard-fought campaign, defeated and conquered the kingdom.

To the west of Dahomey lived the Akan-speakers, a large group inhabiting the coastal plains of the Gold Coast and the rich forest region immediately inland, part of which was one of the most important sources of gold in West Africa. Towards the end of the seventeenth century the Oyoko clan, one of the many groups into which the Akan were divided politically and by lineage, moved north from the southern forests around the river Pra to found six 'city' states in the Kwaman forest, a gold-mining area.

These six little towns formed the nucleus of the Asante kingdom, centred on Kumasi. They were situated in the middle of an already prosperous country, rich in produce and trade—one of the 'suburbs' of Kumasi, Tafo, for instance, itself dated back to the sixteenth century. This town had been instrumental in diverting some of the gold trade from the forest region south to the Europeans on the coast, away from the time-honoured northern route to the Sudanic kingdoms and across the Sahara. Kumasi was at the meeting-point of these two trading systems, which competed both for slaves and for gold.

From the rich heartlands of Asante, Kumasi was connected by roads or paths to all the leading provinces. Four of these royal roads, which were constructed and maintained by the central government of Asante, radiated in a southwards direction, towards the European factory-forts on the coast. The other four went northwards, one linking Asante with the Dyula trading system at Bondoukou, another ultimately reaching Jenné, another going to Gao, and the fourth going in the direction of Hausaland.

On page 48. To the west of the empires of Benin and Oyo was the savannah kingdom of Dahomey, which was at the height of its power in the eighteenth century. Inhabited by the Fon, Dahomey was a highly centralized, militarist state, whose armies were dreaded by all its neighbours. The corps of women soldiers, known to Europeans as Amazons, was particularly ferocious. This almost life-size altar image is of the cult god Gu, to whom was attributed the ultimate power in life and death. It is made from hammered brass plates and is probably from the palace of King Behanzin, Dahomey.

The Oyoko clansmen could therefore exploit a long-existing network of trade and politics. By skilfully manipulating this system, by diplomacy and the prudent use of military pressure, the Asante kings built up an area of wider and wider influence. Between the heartlands around Kumasi and the European 'factories' on the coast, however, lay another and more powerful Akan state, Denkyira, which acted with extreme harshness towards its neighbours, reducing many of them to slavery. Denkyira prevented the Oyoko and other little states of the Kwaman forest from reaching the coast, and it was largely common action in the face of their enemy that persuaded these states to form a united front.

Asante was thus a union of many Akan kingdoms, a kind of federal state, set up in about 1695 by Osei Tutu, the king of Kumasi. Acting closely with one of the important high priests of the region, Okomfo Anokye, Osei Tutu called the people of all those states friendly to the Oyoko clan to an immense assembly at Kumasi. Okomfo Anokye declared that Osei Tutu had a divine mission to weld the Asante and related peoples into a mighty empire.

As a symbol which could bind these states together permanently under the leadership of Kumasi, Osei Tutu and Okomfo Anokye produced a Golden Stool which was to be revered and sacrosanct. A stool was a long-accepted mark of political authority among the Akan, and the priest is said to have brought this Golden Stool down from the sky 'in a black cloud and amidst rumblings'. He then announced to the multitude that the stool embodied the soul and unity of the Asante people. The Golden Stool was never to be lost, the kinship group of Osei Tutu was for ever to be recognized as the head of the Asante Union, and all previous symbols of political authority were to be buried. If it were lost or dishonoured, misfortune would fall on the Asante. The Golden Stool stood forever as the symbol of the *asantehene*, the Asante emperor; it was not used as a seat, even at coronations.

Left : Fon woodcarving of a lion from the palace of the Dahomey kings at Abomey. Dating from the nineteenth century, this carving was therefore made towards the end of the independence of the kingdom.

Right : An Asante soul-bearer's badge, worn by the priests who accompanied the asantehene, and who carried the Golden Stool. Asante was one of the main producers of gold in West Africa, and many splendid gold ornaments and other objects were made by the emperor's artists. This example is particularly fine. It was made by pouring liquid gold into a clay shell surrounding a carved wax matrix, through only one aperture. The intricate design had to be incised on the wax, and then the gold poured in so that no one part would solidify before another.

Left : Solid gold head from Asante, modern Ghana. This was probably an ornament originally attached to a royal stool, or perhaps even the Golden Stool, symbol of the Asante emperor. It represents the head of an important enemy —possibly with spiritual powers—killed in battle.

Right : Globular hilt ornament of an iron sword buried in the ground at Kumasi, the capital of the Asante union. This was Okomfo Anokye's sword. As high priest of the Akan kingdoms, he drove his sword into the ground with such force that it has remained there ever since, to mark the site of the new imperial city, at the founding of the union of the Akan kingdoms in about 1695. Osei Tutu, King of Kumasi, was proclaimed asantehene or Emperor of Asante by Okomfo Anokye.

The influence of the Asante Union spread far and wide beyond the actual boundaries of the empire. Likewise, Asante cultural influence was widespread. The asantehene sent little stools, staffs and other regalia to tributary or vassal kings and chiefs, and those and other aspects of Akan artistic culture were absorbed by other peoples. On their side, the tributary states sent slaves to Kumasi; these performed work in Asante, but were also exported to the European traders on the Gold Coast.

The *omanhene*, kings of the federated states which made up the Union, had to attend the annual Odwira, or cleansing ceremony, which, as a rite for the dead, cleansed the nation from defilement and purified all ancestral shrines, as well as those dedicated to the national gods. The omanhene also had to send their sons and other relatives to Kumasi, ostensibly to be educated and serve as courtiers, but in effect as hostages for their fathers' good behaviour. By a variety of often quite subtle ways, the asantehene came to wield an immense power, as the British were to learn to their cost in the nineteenth century.

Throughout the southern Sudanic regions, then, West Africa produced a dazzling array of independent states. Each forged its own coherent identity, which could respond to new opportunities as well as resist hostile pressure. Yet within these huge empires there remained dozens of small, individual societies which paid tribute in the form of labour, slaves or agricultural produce, but maintained their own distinctive cultures. Even on this small scale, religion and politics combined to protect the identity of the group with a strong fabric of tradition; and it is to these less flamboyant but more enduring societies that we turn next.

Peoples of the North

They say the houses of Molu in Tomboké are fine,
That the houses of Molu are fine.
In Molu the houses have storeys.
But it is the men who are fine,
Not the storeyed houses!

('Conversations with Ogolemmêli', M. Griaule *An Introduction to Dogon Religious Ideas* London 1965)

The recorded history of West Africa—as of most human societies—is the history of the powerful, of empires and their rulers. Little is recalled of the everyday lives, the aspirations, happiness and suffering of the common men and women, in the cities, the forests or the savannah. Yet the societies which became famous for these political achievements—the Malinke, the Songhay and the Asante—form only a small part of the historical pageant. For more than 2,000 years the vast majority of West Africans lived in small groups, growing their crops or tending their cattle, and developing their own distinctive customs and traditions.

Left : Fulani woman selling milk in Mopti market, Mali. This is a high caste woman, who carries much of her family's wealth around her person ; the hair-rings—not ear-rings—are solid gold. She probably belongs to a pagan or only partly Islamized group of Fulani cattle nomads.

Right : Calabash used for milk by Fulani women. This example comes from Hausaland in northern Nigeria. The intricate designs follow patterns of ideological significance which, in many different forms, are widespread throughout West Africa.

Above : A hump-backed cow of the savannah areas, typical of the great herds of cattle that migrated with the Fulani for many centuries from the west to the east of the Sudanic zone. The cattle of the forest margins further south are a smaller variety, the dwarf short-horn.

Below : Part of a leather camel saddle bag from Mauritania. This is the work of the Berber 'Moors' who roamed as nomads in the arid semi-desert country to the north of the Senegal river. The patterns on the saddle bag are strongly influenced by Islamic designs.

The large and spectacular kingdoms and empires never occupied the whole of the immense territory of West Africa. There were many peoples and societies who were not included in them, or who were only involved peripherally. Yet these peoples possessed a dynamic, rich culture and history, even if their histories are not as easy to distinguish as those of the great kingdoms. In some cases these smaller, independent societies possessed a richer and more diverse culture than the inhabitants of the kingdoms, perhaps because the latter were involved in paying tribute to their masters. Amongst the many diverse cultures that developed in the Sudanic region of the north perhaps the most diverse in life-style, cultural beliefs and history were the Dogon, who remained settled in their particular and rather special environment for many hundreds of years, and the nomadic Fulani.

The cattle-herding Fulani were the great wandering people of West Africa, who over the course of a comparatively short period of time migrated eastwards from near the Atlantic coast of Senegal to the area around Lake Chad and beyond. As cattle-keepers and nomads the Fulani contrast vividly with most other West African peoples, who were content to remain more or less at their place of birth. Although the Mande-speaking groups spread across the west, this happened extremely slowly, and only a few societies specializing in trade, such as the Dyula and the Hausa, moved far afield. Even the steady process of migration from the savannah to the southern rain forests was almost imperceptible, an endless sequence of small-scale tribal movements.

The history of the Fulani is dominated by population movements right from their origins. They provide one of the few examples in West Africa of the mixing of two racial groups, as distinct from ethnic or tribal groups. On one side they are descended from the Negro Tukulor of the Senegal; on the other, they descend from Caucasoid Berbers who mingled with the Tukulor when they moved south from the Sahara. The Tukulor were related linguistically to the Serer and Wolof peoples; their present name, significantly, is thought to be a corruption of the English 'two colours'.

In the eleventh century the Tukulor were forced to give up their territory north of the Senegal river to the Berbers, who were migrating across the Sahara from Morocco. These Berbers were pastoralists—indeed the herdsmen who appear in the Saharan rock paintings might well have been their ancestors. The people they mixed with, and whose Negro language came to predominate, soon took up their cattle-keeping way of life. The ruling family of the Tukulor converted enthusiastically to the Islam introduced by some of the invading Berbers; indeed, they were amongst the first rulers of black West Africa to do so. Previously the Tukulor had traced their descent through the wife's family, or by matrilineage, and a young husband went to live in the village or small riverside town of his newly acquired maternal uncle. Under the influence of Islam and of Berber society, the Tukulor gradually changed over to patrilineal descent, and the wife would come to live at the village of her father-in-law. But over the centuries the Tukulor have retained several other Berber customs. For example, a bride's parents give their daughter a dowry in the form of cattle or pigs. In most Negro societies it is the man who has to bring a bride price to the girl's parents, as compensation for the family's economic loss.

Although the Tukulor north of the Senegal had been driven out of their land, in the fertile valley of the river they were strong enough to withstand Berber pressure. The Berbers then turned from military conquest to economic penetration, moving their herds into lands less suited to agriculture. There was little room for grazing on the well-watered land along the Senegal but south of the river the open savannah of Futa Toro offered excellent pasturage, and was only sparsely occupied because the ground was less fertile and the water more scarce. Here the Berber nomads established themselves and flourished. Thus it was here, too, on Futa Toro, that the Fulani emerged as a distinct West African people. For, although the Berbers were fiercely independent in spirit, they were isolated from

Right : Intricately designed, colourful matting made by the Wogo people of Tillaberi on the Niger river in Niger. The Wogo, like the Fulani and Tuareg, are nomadic. These mattings are used to erect tents for special occasions, such as weddings and political or religious ceremonies.

their kinsmen in Mauritania and subject to varying degrees of Tukulor control. Gradually they adopted the Tukulor language and even intermarried with them to some extent. Nevertheless, the pastoral population of the Futa Toro remained mostly Caucasoid—straight-nosed, straighthaired, thin-lipped, wiry, copper- or bronze-complexioned—while the sedentary farmers and townsfolk along the Senegal were mainly Negroid.

As time went on, these physical distinctions were reinforced by other contrasting characteristics. The Caucasoid Fulani remained nomadic; they were normally indifferent as Muslims and often down-to-earth pagans; they were generally men of peace who accommodated themselves to their neighbours, and they had no political organization above the level of the cattle band and its elders. The Negro Fulani, on the other hand, were cultivators living in villages or small towns, although adverse conditions sometimes forced them to become nomadic; they tended to be fanatic Muslims, committed to proselytizing their faith, and eager supporters of the *jihad* or holy war against pagans and back-sliding Muslims.

The nomads were constantly on the move, spreading eastwards from the Futa Toro, in search of pasture for their herds. They slowly became an accepted feature across the whole of the Sudanic region. Socially and culturally, they kept themselves to themselves—their way of life was extremely demanding, and imposed strict limits. For the greater part of the year they were on the move, taking their herds from dry season to wet season pastures. At the height of the rains they would establish a camp, but this was always a temporary settlement and as soon as the rains eased up they would be off in search of new grazing lands. The Fulani nomads lived for, with and by their cattle: they had no desire for power or displays of material wealth; most of them in fact were poor, and European visitors would later compare them to the gypsies of their own continent.

57

Above : A Peul woman from north Niger with her distinctive coiffure. The tribal marks on her face show that she belongs to the nomadic Peul, who call themselves Boroboro (a subdivision of the Fulani).

Below : A hut in a Zerma village compound, raised above the ground to make it safe against snakes, rats and mosquitoes.

In the nomads' eyes this was the only way to live. They held themselves aloof from the settled population, whom they came to regard as racially and culturally inferior. Although they adopted many of the farmers' social institutions, they retained their own language, traditions and superstitions. Over the years the nomads were more influenced by Islam, but they were never more than nominal Muslims. This lax attitude to religion must have shocked their stricter brethren, but the demands of pastoralism made it difficult for them to follow many of the tenets of Islam. The segregation and seclusion of women was impractical, for the work done by women was essential for survival. Ritual ablutions and prayers five times a day were scarcely compatible with watching over the herds.

In matters of marriage and divorce the nomads ignored Islamic law completely. In some of the clans it was common practice for a married woman to run away with her lover, and this new 'marriage' would be accepted by the clan if she had managed to reach the man's hut without being caught by the husband. When a fight broke out and the husband was the victor, he could take his wife back by force. Otherwise the new husband compensated the former husband with the same number of cattle as in the original bride price.

The life of a cattle herdsman, dependent for survival on the safety and well-being of the herd, was not easy, and despite their slight build, the Fulani were both tough and courageous. *Soro*, a ceremony in which Fulani youths proved their manhood and their readiness for marriage, was a way of ensuring the continued strength of the group. Each youth was beaten on the chest or back with a heavy stick—usually two or three times. If a healthy young man did not go through with the soro ceremony he would be considered a coward and this would lessen his marriage chances. He was expected to show no sign of pain, but to take the beating without flinching or crying out. Often he would hold up a mirror and gaze at his reflection, ensuring that he did not change his expression. The beating invariably

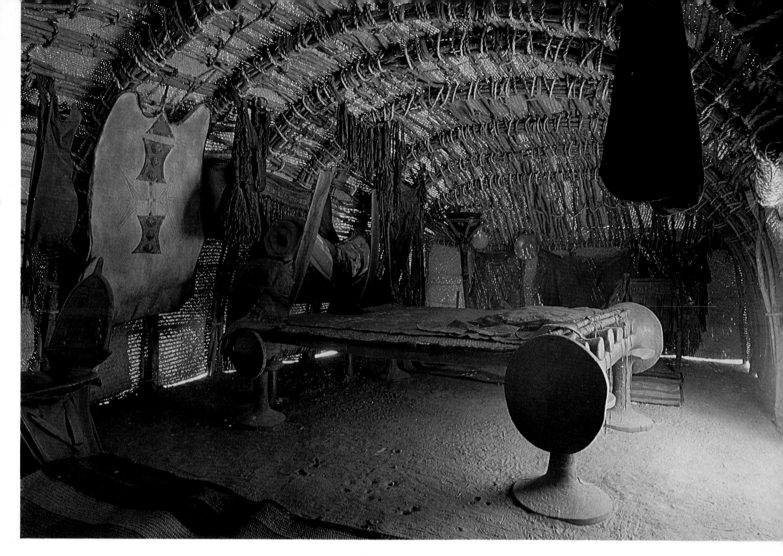

resulted in large weals, which might be there for life, and Fulani men were proud of this scarring, for it was visible proof of their strength and bravery.

Despite this ritual, Fulani daily life was characterized by neither violence nor aggression, and soro played only a small part in their culture. With their cattle they were gentle, almost devoted. Fulani cows could not have been described as tame, yet even small boys knew how to keep a large herd under control. They knew each beast individually and named them according to their markings and colouring. The Fulani rarely ate meat, for that would mean reducing their stock; instead they lived on milk and butter. The cows were such an integral part of Fulani society that they were often given clan names. A man who committed a crime or offended the clan was punished by having his cattle taken away from him.

The pastoral Fulani travelled in bands which often comprised no more than the nuclear family of parents and children. They lived in temporary camps consisting of a cluster of tents which could be collapsed and moved, often surrounded by a thorn hedge; these also provided the enclosures or kraals in which cattle were kept at night. The huts were usually beehive-shaped, with a framework of poles covered with mats, leaves or grass.

These nomads did not migrate alone but they were always accompanied by at least some of their settled and more Negroid kinsfolk—better educated, more sophisticated in political matters, and far less tolerant of the infidel. The sedentary Fulani lived in permanent villages or towns, with cone-shaped thatched houses built from mud or sun-dried brick, many with intricate passages and interior courtyards, closely packed one against another, and often surrounded by a wall or stockade.

As herdsmen, the Fulani borrowed most of their cultural and social institutions from neighbouring peoples, notably the Soninke and the Mande; they were even divided into four main clans like the Mande, from whom they may have borrowed the system. But while the nomads were basically egalitarian, though with variations of wealth, their sedentary kin

Above: Interior of a Tuareg tent house, with a large bed and a rug in the foreground. This one is at Air, a mountainous region deep in the Sahara in Niger, and the site of an ancient Tuareg sultanate.

Below: A Tuareg shield from Air, called 'worudwadji' (the name of the animal from which the skin comes), incised with an intricate design. It is used by the Tuareg when fighting or hunting.

Above : A miniature Koran from Hausa, northern Nigeria, dating from the late seventeenth or early eighteenth century. The decoration shows the typical Islamic magic design that accompanied the penetration of Islam to the south of the Sahara (see also p. 18).

were divided into nobles, commoners, serfs and slaves as well as into castes or clans of clerics, bards (called *griots*) and skilled artisans—sculptors and metal-workers—who married only among themselves.

In time these 'better clan' Fulani became the dominant military and political group throughout the western Sudan. From the seventeenth century onwards there was a general impoverishment in the whole region. The Muslim Fulani became more sharply distinguished from the ordinary people, and, as privileged classes, sought a form of wealth which was both easy to keep and easy to convert. In many cases, the form they chose was cattle. For not only were the Fulani acknowledged experts in the care of cattle, but they were also in sole charge of this desirable commodity. They were, however, still tainted with the general disdain felt by their neighbours for all Fulani. It was Islam that enabled them to gain cohesion, and to force themselves into dominant roles, socially as well as economically.

A firm caste system developed. At the top were the great Fulani lords— urban dwellers, landlords and military men. Then there were groups who acted as intermediaries, emissaries and functionaries to all the other caste groups, and to neighbouring peoples. Next in importance were the cultivators, many of whom used various ways to obtain exemption from actual work in the fields. Further down the hierarchy of the caste system were the specialists—butchers, blacksmiths, jewellers, wood-workers or joiners (who were regarded as magicians), leather-workers, weavers and cobblers. At the bottom of the list were the lowly family cattlemen.

Towards the end of the seventeenth century Islam enjoyed a spectacular revival throughout the western Sudan, influenced by similar movements in North Africa and elsewhere in the Muslim world. This Islamic fervour, which continued throughout the eighteenth century before reaching a peak in the early nineteenth, impressed the Fulani in an important and wholly new manner. For now even the herdsmen were caught up in the ardours of Islam and converted to the religion. This was to have a revolutionary effect.

The will for dominance amongst the higher caste Fulani now took the form of a jihad. This was fought not just against pagan infidels, but more frequently against Muslim townsmen and peasants who, in the estimation of the Fulani, were backsliders in the faith. The jihad was the inspiration for a new bout of territorial expansion. From Masina, their main centre in the seventeenth century, the Fulani moved in many directions. They partly retraced their steps westwards to the southern banks of the Senegal, where they set up a state called Futa Toro; they moved eastwards into Hausaland and Nupe, in modern Nigeria; and they migrated south-west, to the mountains of Futa Jallon.

As usual, the pastoralists were accompanied by Muslim clerics who encouraged their leaders to establish a base town, to which the heads of the Fulani clans could come to discuss internal affairs. There the clerics established Koranic schools. At Futa Jallon it so happened that the interests of pastoralists and clerics coincided, and two leaders emerged— the pious Muslim Ibrahim Musa and the warrior Ibrahim Sori. The nomad chieftains aimed to set up a Muslim state, so in 1725 Ibrahim Musa launched his jihad against the local Dialonke people. His extended campaign was not very successful, however, and when he died in 1751 the jihad was on the verge of failure. At that point the Fulani assembly elected Ibrahim Sori as their war leader, and by the time he died in 1784 he had won Futa Jallon for the Fulani and for Islam.

The Muslim theocracy which emerged there was both idealistic and democratic in its early days. A system of joint rule was adapted, with one *al-mami*, or leader, elected every two years, the candidates alternating between the families and supporters of Ibrahim Musa and Ibrahim Sori. Provincial, district and local administration, religious as well as political, was carefully worked out. The whole system was understood to be dominated by the word of Allah, the One God.

Similar states developed in Futa Toro (with Tukulor clerics playing a

Right : A Hausa village compound. Looking out from the cool of the compound gateway, which also acts as a lobby to the compound and as the house of the head of the family. Both the house and the bedstead are made out of dried mud.

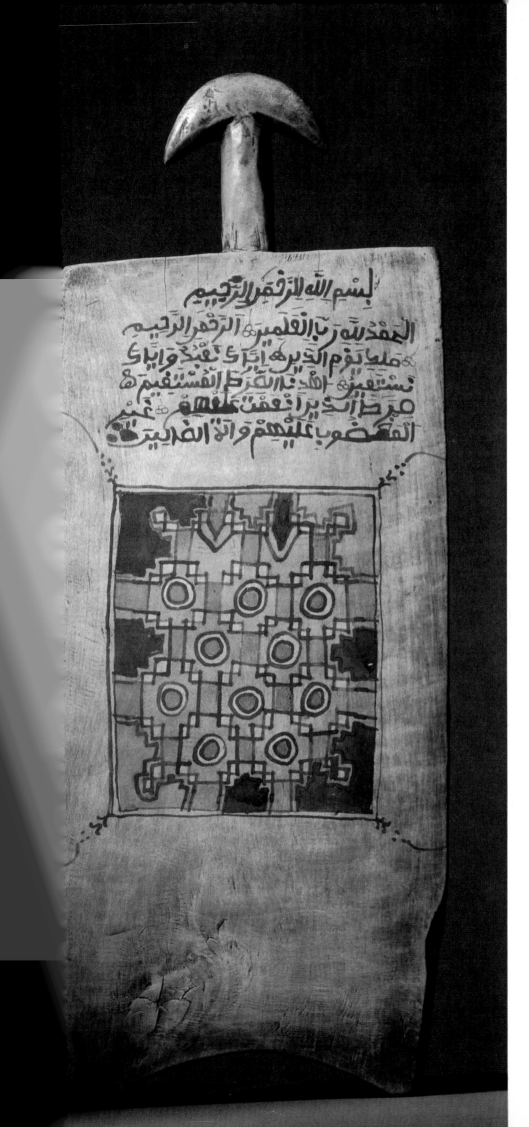

Left : A wooden board from Hausaland,
with a sacred Arabic text from the Koran.
Such boards were used in the Islamic
schools, and on successful completion of
studies were inscribed with ' Allon sabka da
Zayyana', which was not deleted, as the
lessons previously had been. The board is
50 cm (20 in) long.

Right : A Dogon iron staff depicting a
human figure with a bow. The Dogon
belonged to a large group called Voltaic
peoples, who lived south of the great Niger
bend, in the basin created by the Black and
White Volta rivers. Together with other
Voltaic people such as the Senufo and
Mossi, and Mande people such as the
Bambara, they developed a highly
stylized art form, very different from that
of, for instance, the Benin and Ife forms.
It was extremely linear and often full of
movement. This iron figure seems to be both
weightless and tense. It is characteristic of
much of Dogon art, which expresses their
cosmology—the relation of man to the spirit
world of the gods. It is a reduction of an
idea of man to its essentials.

leading role) and elsewhere in the western Sudan. The British traveller Mungo Park visited Bondu, in the grassland north-west of Futa Jallon, at the end of the eighteenth century. He was most hospitably received by the king, who lived in an assembly of clay-built houses surrounded by a hill wall. The king introduced Park to his wives, who found their first sight of a European very entertaining—they teased him about the whiteness of his skin and the size of his nose, saying that both were artificial. Park found Bondu prosperous and at peace; religious persecution was unknown. The state was provided with village schools; the children were well-behaved, healthy and attentive. The cattle-breeders of the countryside were wealthy 'and enjoy the necessaries of life in a high degree'.

The most awesome jihads, and those with the most widespread repercussions, took place in the nineteenth century. The first was led by Uthman dan Fodio, a Fulani cleric who raised the standard of revolt in 1804. Within a few years, his massed cavalry conquered most of Hausaland, the northern half of modern Nigeria, and far beyond. The Fulani *amirs*, or military commanders, took over from the Hausa aristocracy as the political leaders of the whole area. In 1817 Uthman's son proclaimed the Sultanate of Sokoto, which remained in being until the British occupation at the end of the nineteenth century.

One of Uthman's followers, Ahmadu Lobo, led a Fulani army westwards to conquer Masina on the middle Niger. Then Umar, a cleric from Futa Toro, called al-Hajj because he undertook the pilgrimage to Mecca, launched from Futa Jallon what was perhaps the fiercest of all jihads. Many of these powerful Muslim states came into violent conflict with the invading Europeans towards the end of the nineteenth century; indeed, the French took more than two decades of heavy fighting to overthrow al-Hajj Umar's Muslim empire.

Yet while the revolutionary power of Allah fuelled the expansionist energies of the Fulani, other peoples of the savannah took different paths and developed quite different societies. Typical in many respects of these were the Dogon, a pantheistic people, acutely conscious of the natural world, inward-looking, and with a world view of exceptional complexity. Unlike the nomadic Fulani they were very securely settled. Their whole complex way of life and culture was fixed firmly in their attachment to their land—the land of their spirits, gods and ancestors.

Dogon country divides fairly naturally into three basic parts: a plain, a cliff-like escarpment and a plateau. The plain and most of the plateau are thinly wooded, but the relief of the plateau is tortuous. It is furrowed by numerous valleys from which a great number of torrents fall southwards in spectacular waterfalls, towards the river Gordo, while other streams, with a slower fall, flowed eastwards towards the Niger. The plateau consists of massive layers of sandstone. At the escarpment great chunks of rock fall away regularly, shattering into boulders.

The Dogon moved into this remarkable country from the west, possibly from the Mande dispersal area. They were by no means the first occupants of Dogonland. Myths tell of a race of little folk called the Andumbala, who lived on the cliffs of the escarpment from very early times. They were superseded by tall men, the Tellem, whom the Dogon seem to have pushed out in turn, on to the plains, possibly in the fifteenth century.

Like many other peoples in Africa, the Dogon were originally hunters and must have been drawn to the large herds of game which lived on the plains. But they could not resist the strange cliffs and plateau country, and in time most of the Dogon left the uncertainty of the open plains and moulded their lives to the mysterious and ambiguous new environment. They developed an immensely complex set of religious and philosophical ideas—a cosmology—to account for their lives, habits, culture and rituals, and for the physical setting against which these were enacted.

The Dogon reflected deeply on their lives. They lived a simple farming life, following the skills of this kind of existence, such as agriculture and

On page 64 : *A Dogon village viewed from a cave in the cliff-face escarpment. The flat-roofed houses, some with small conical towers, are clustered close together, with narrow alleys between. In the foreground, at the foot of the escarpment, are great boulders which have fallen from the cliff. Scattered around are baobab trees. The plain beyond is now almost treeless; in former days it was well wooded. Far from the Dogon ideal, this village appears to be haphazard.*

On page 65 : *Another Dogon village nestling under a huge overhanging cliff, which is pocked with caves. The dried mud houses are built on a wooden framework which is such a common feature of the Sudanic region. On the wall of one house in the centre of the picture is a relief of a lizard, one of the most characteristic symbolic representations of the Dogon people.*

weaving and smithing, in a way which might be regarded as primitive. But all were efficient in the context of Dogon society and their environment, and had a rich, hidden significance.

Religious ceremonies and gestures, whether spectacular or secret, were of an extreme subtlety in their implications and generally incomprehensible to outsiders. The smallest everyday object could reveal in its form or decoration the conscious reflection of a complex cosmology: a checkered coverlet or garment was a text in which the woven designs constituted signs expressed by its makers and known to initiates. When turned upside down, a basket for bringing in the harvest depicted the rainbow on which humanity descended from the heavens to earth: its square base connoted space, and its four corners the cardinal points of the compass. The paintings on a totemic sanctuary, made at different periods of the year with materials derived from different cereals, were both a writing and a form of numeration. The sacrifice of a humble chicken, when accompanied by the necessary and effective ritual gestures, recalled the origins and functioning of the universe.

The Dogon had systems of divination and calculation which ran into thousands of signs, and these were used in their own sciences of astronomy and calendrical measurement. They also developed an extensive anatomical and physiological knowledge, and a systematic pharmacopoeia. Textiles, games, rites, and the manifestations of nature, including plants, animals and insects, were distributed in categories which were further divided, numerically expressed and related one to another. The political and religious authority of the chiefs, the family system and juridical rights,

indeed, all the activities of daily life, were ultimately based on these principles, as well as the usual African resort to oracles.

The extent to which their spiritual view of life permeated their physical surroundings is shown dramatically by the arrangement of buildings in villages, and of rooms and other features in individual homesteads. Twins occupied a crucial position in their thinking, being used to explain dualities such as male and female, and villages accordingly were often twinned, one being on the plateau above the escarpment, the other among the rocks at the foot of the almost vertical cliff.

Villages consisted of tangles of dwellings surrounded by granaries and outbuildings. An ideal village would extend from north to south like the body of a man lying on his back. The head was the village council house, built on the chief square, which was the symbol of the primal field, cultivated by the earliest Dogon. On the north side of the chief square was the smithy—the smith being the bringer of civilization. To the east and west were houses where the women were secluded during menstruation; these were round like wombs and represented the hands of the village. The larger family houses were its chest and belly; the communal altars at the south of the village were its feet.

In the centre of the village were placed the stones for crushing the fruit of the *hannea acida* tree, from which the Dogon obtained most of their precious oil. These represented the female sexual parts of the village; beside them was the foundation altar, which was its male sex organ. Out of respect for the women this altar was frequently erected outside the confines of the village.

Ideally, like the village as a whole, individual buildings were laid out in a way determined by the Dogon view of creation. The Dogon creation myths specify eight ancestors who, after a time in human form, were transformed into water spirits. The man's shelter and meeting house, which was generally built in the centre of a village, had eight supports, representing these ancestors. The ground plan of these eight pillars resembled a serpent coiled along a broken line and surrounding the symbols of the seventh ancestor, the Master of Speech, and the eighth ancestor, who was the Word itself.

These ancestors were procreated by twin spirits, called Nummo, who themselves were the offspring of God, Amma. Amma created the universe, including the earth, which he made from a lump of clay. The clay spread and fell on the north, which was the top of the world, and from there stretched out to the south, which was the bottom. It extended east and west with separate members.

The earth was a female body, which lay flat, face upwards, in a line from north to south. Its sexual organ was an anthill and its clitoris a termite hill. After first excising the termite-hill or clitoris, Amma had had intercourse with his world-woman which had led to the formation of the Nummo twins, half human and half serpent. After a number of adventures and misadventures, they procreated the ancestral men.

Inside each house, the rooms represented the caves, or sections of the world inhabited by mankind. The vestibule, which belonged to the master of the house, represented the male partner of the couple, the outside door being his sexual organ. The big central room was the domain and symbol of the woman; the store-rooms each side were her arms, and the communicating door her sexual parts. The central room and the store-rooms together represented the woman lying on her back with outstretched arms, the door open and the woman ready for intercourse. The room at the back, which contained the hearth and looked out on to the flat roof, showed the breathing of the woman, who lay in the central chamber. The ceiling above her symbolized the man, its beams representing his skeleton; their breath found its outlet through the opening above. The four upright posts were the couple's arms—those of the woman supporting the man, who rested his own on the ground. When a child was born, the woman in labour was seated on a stool in the middle of the room, her back to the north, and

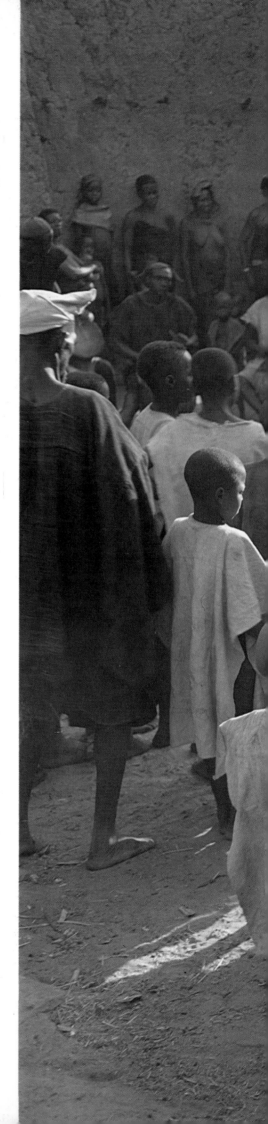

On page 67 : A funeral ceremony in a Dogon village in front of the house of the deceased. People come from all over Dogon country with gifts, chiefly of food. They dance before the close relatives of the deceased, and guns are fired and weapons brandished. Most funerals take place in March and April, the 'months of dying'.

supported by other women. The infant was delivered on the ground and took possession of its soul in the place where it was conceived.

The earthen platform that served as a bed lay north-south and the couple slept on it with their heads to the north, like the house itself, whose front wall was its face. The man lay on his right side facing west, and the woman on her left side facing east, the positions they would occupy in the grave. The man touched the woman with his left hand, never with his right; the woman touched the man with her right.

Under the bed were put all the seeds for sowing except cotton seeds, which were placed on the lintel of the second door, symbol of the female sex. In sexual intercourse the man was sowing; he was like a water spirit causing fertilizing rain to fall on the earth and on the woman who represented the sown seeds. When the couple lay with a covering over them, as in death, the bed became a symbol of the grave. The seeds were made to germinate, and children were procreated, by the action of the couple lying under the funeral pall, in itself a symbol of numerous lineages and cultivated lands.

This rich but everyday symbolism is only possible in such a settled and secure society. The Dogon may have originally entered their weird homelands in search of refuge, and certainly, over the centuries, they avoided conquest by all the powerful empires which threatened them—Ghana, Mali and Songhay. Yet their greatest sanctuary was their spiritual knowledge, which gave them a certainty and confidence unknown to other societies. Variations of their mythology are common in West Africa, but the Dogon, even more than other peoples, developed a unifying conception of their world and of the nature of mankind. Where the Fulani found confidence in Islam, the Dogon, like many other sedentary people of the north, drew from their own deep inner resources.

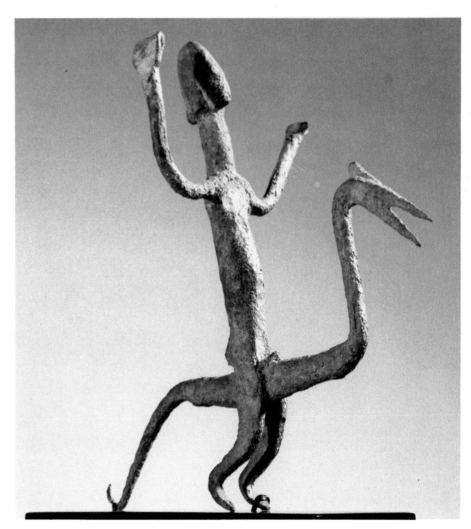

Left : The men's council chamber of a Dogon village. Great wooden pillars support the heavy roof and are decorated with breasts—the female principle, as opposed to the lizard, which is the male principle. Constructed on a bare rock floor, the houses reserved for the males have a low roof of layers of reed which may be up to 3 m (10 ft) thick. This insulates against the heat, and it is always cool inside.

Right: A wrought-iron Bambara image of a mythical monster and its anthropomorhized rider.

Peoples of the South

Our land is uncommonly rich and fruitful, and produces all kinds of vegetables in great abundance. We have plants of Italian corn, and vast quantities of cotton and tobacco. We have spices of various kinds, particularly pepper; and a variety of delicious fruits, together with gums and honey in great abundance. All our work is to improve these blessings of nature. Agriculture is our chief employment; and everyone, even the children and women, are engaged on it. The benefits of such a way of living are felt by us in the general healthiness of the people, and in their vigour and strength.

(The Interesting Narrative of the Life of Olandah Equiano or Gustavus Vassa, the African, written by himself London 1789)

In the dense tropical rain forests behind the mangrove swamps, long tidal creeks and numerous islands of the huge Niger delta, and in the wooded savannah north of the forest edge, were some of the most densely populated regions of West Africa. To the west of the river were the Edo and the Yoruba, with their highly organized city states and kingdoms; to the east lived the Ibo and other related peoples, who, in contrast, enjoyed a less centralized, more democratic way of life. In these societies every man had an inalienable right to voice his opinion on public affairs at the village assembly, and any innovation which might deprive citizens of their right to share in decision-making was strongly resisted.

In spite of the huge impact of the trans-Atlantic slave trade in the seventeenth century, which caused many peoples of the delta swamps to set up tightly organized states, the Ibo and their neighbours in the forest hinterland remained tenaciously committed to their village democracies. This was a real achievement in the face of the extensive slaving they had to endure.

The availability of food crops helped make the Ibo societies resilient to these pressures. The natural crops of the forest—including cotton, earth peas, fluted pumpkins, gourds, okra and sesame—were all, and especially Guinea yams and oil palms, gathered from earliest times and cultivated to supplement basic fishing and hunting. Some Sudanic food crops penetrated into the forest lands from the north at an early period, but the main ones, sorghum and millet, were not well suited to the conditions of the tropical forests, and only acquired some ritual significance.

A major demographic change amongst the forest peoples seems to have been caused around 2,000 years ago when food crops were introduced from Asia, particularly from the Malay peninsula. Larger, more nutritious yams

71

and taro were particularly easily grown in local conditions, while bananas, another Asian food, flourished in the Cameroun region, and the population rocketed with these new foods. The introduction of cultivated plants from Brazil and the West Indies after 1500 provided a further enrichment of the subsistence economy. Peppers, pineapples, pumpkins, squash, sweet potatoes, tobacco and tomatoes spread widely, and maize, manioc and peanuts became staple crops.

Many of the forest crops were in fruit nearly all the year round, and production was fairly easy, although a great deal of thought and effort had to go into maintaining the fertility of the unstable soils. But the fast-growing and ever-encroaching forest continued to dominate the people's lives; it determined their settlement patterns and played a vital part in shaping their distinctive cultures. Thus when the Ibo cleared areas of the forest, they used every possible inch of fertile land to cultivate small farms. They hacked narrow, twisting paths which weaved their way from compound to compound, and led from the compounds to the market and the central meeting place, to the shrine of the local deity, and to other villages. And eventually, despite the forest, Iboland became the most densely populated area of West Africa.

Many of the Ibo kept livestock, particularly cattle, but also goats, sheep, dogs and chickens, although the tropical conditions (especially the prevalence of tsetse fly) were often unsuitable for the larger domestic animals. Local trade and handicraft industries were highly developed, and complicated systems of markets emerged. The Ibo man hunted, cleared the land for agriculture, and did most of the fishing, while the women cultivated and harvested the crops, and marketed the surpluses.

Above left : Raffia cloth made by the Baule of the Ivory Coast. This tie-dyed cloth was highly appreciated for its colourful effect and surface texture of permanent wrinkles.

Above : A wooden calabash stopper representing the head of a young woman with a prominent hairstyle.

Right : An Ibo boy. The Ibo live in what is probably the densest African forest. Even small boys are put to work gathering the useful products of the forest, in this case fodder.

On page 70 : Grinding millet in Miango village in the wooded savannah of Nigeria. The compound is surrounded by a high fence, for privacy, and to keep out marauding animals. This village is on the Jos plateau.

Unlike the Yoruba to the west of the Niger, the Ibo have no complex or comprehensive traditions of origin. But in historical times—as far as they are concerned, since about 1400—they have been divided into five large groups who have differed to some extent in language, work patterns and religion. These five groups were the northern Onitisha or Nri Awka Ibo; the southern or Owerri Ibo; the western Ibo; the eastern or Cross River Ibo; and the north-eastern or Ogoja Ibo.

Their types of government are very ancient and follow the same basic principles. Most Ibo have governed themselves without allowing powerful chiefs or kings to merge, but some, like those of Nri Awka near the Niger, had their own little kings, while others—the Cross River Ibo of the eastern delta, for instance—made use of councils of elders, village headmen, and other groups of prominent local people. But by and large theirs was a segmentary society, both highly developed and successful, in which power was vested in the people. Authority was questioned, and individual effort and competition were encouraged. The Ibo were probably the most democratic people in West Africa.

The basic social and political unit was the village, which managed its own affairs, but which had strong ties with other villages, often forming part of a larger group. Every village, or group of villages, had craftsmen skilled in weaving, wood-working and metal-working, and all were connected by paths and trade routes through the forest. At the centre of a group of villages was a market and a meeting place where a clan could assemble to thrash out a dispute over land or among warring factions of a family.

Each village in a group believed in a communal charter, now thought to be mythical, tracing common descent from a founding ancestor. His sons were held to have established the constituent villages of the group and all the lineages in a village were believed to have descended from one son. Kinship links were sometimes emphasized to create special relationships with neighbouring village-groups, and because of their close ties the men of a village had to go outside it to find their wives.

Administration of justice was democratic and flexible. The Ibo believed that their gods and ancestors were directly involved in the running of village affairs, and whenever important judicial or legislative decisions had to be made, supernatural sanction was sought. At such times leading members of the clan masqueraded as *egwugwu*, the ancestral spirits, whose decisions could not be questioned. Since the ancestors were regarded as the guardians of morality, they could publicly chastise or punish a wrong-doer; the shame and fear this brought was likely to discourage a repetition of the offence.

Egwugwu appear in *Things Fall Apart*, Chinua Achebe's novel of Ibo village life—first to judge an unresolved family dispute and later to attend the funeral of a prominent clansman. 'The egwugwu with the springy walk was one of the dead fathers of the clan. He looked terrible with the smoked raffia body, a huge wooden face painted white except for the round hollow eyes and the charred teeth that were as big as a man's finger. On his head were two powerful horns.' Their presence at funerals was a reminder that the land of the living was close to the land of the dead. 'There was a coming and going between them, especially at funerals and also when an old man died, because an old man was very close to the ancestors.'

In day-to-day matters government was through village assemblies and village-group councils. The former were presided over by lineage heads, who were regarded as the earthly representatives of the lineage ancestors. They had considerable moral authority, but their power was controlled by the will of the assembly. Every man had the right to speak and the lineage heads could not act without a consensus of opinion. Village-group councils were composed of the heads of lineages, each holding an *oto* staff—the symbol of their ancestor—and other wealthy or influential men. The man who held the senior oto of the group of villages was regarded as a titular 'father', but had no political powers other than those given to any elder.

Above : A wooden loom heddle pulley made by the Gwa peoples of the coastal lagoons of the Ivory Coast. In weaving, a heddle separates the warp threads into two sets so as to allow passage of the shuttle bearing the weft.

A system of age grades provided the Ibo with social cohesion and authority. Grading divided adult males into elders, middle-aged, sometimes warriors, and young adults. An individual moved from one grade to another as he advanced in years. In any one village the young men did the heavy work (or shared this with the women), fought as warriors when necessary, often voiced dissatisfaction about the state of village life, and generally started most quarrels. The elders acted as advisers on the conduct of public works and warfare, moderated village affairs, settled quarrels and legal disputes, and oversaw religious and ritual ceremonies.

Each man was judged by his achievements. His position in the clan was not determined by birth; he could rise to a position of eminence by becoming wealthy or through his record of service to his clan. Because of fear of the forest, people were reluctant to stray into it alone. The forest then made for an open and communal style of life, and the support and respect of the community were all-important to an ambitious man. Neighbours were more than neighbours: they were of the same family, the same clan, sharing ancestors and a guardian deity.

A family always had strong links with villages other than its own. As a man was expected to marry outside his own village, he would enter into a new and binding relationship with his wife's lineage kin. Ibo society was polygamous, especially for the prosperous who had more wives the richer they were, and these marriage ties between villages greatly facilitated trading and social contacts and reduced the likelihood of inter-village feuds.

An Ibo man was unquestionably the head of his household. The children belonged to him. His wives were under his protection and were not expected to challenge his authority. Nevertheless, Ibo women had greater freedom and more influence in their society than many other women in West Africa, particularly those in Muslim-dominated areas. They had equal rights where divorce was concerned, and could divorce their husbands for sterility, cruelty, desertion or adultery. They could also leave men who were of poor character or thieves.

A man's first wife was regarded as the senior wife, and subsequent wives had to respect her position of authority in the household. In turn, a man was expected to divide his time equally between his wives, and not to show favouritism before them. Sexual jealousy was uncommon; where rivalry did occur, it was usually over children—when one wife had borne no sons, or when one child was given more attention by the father than were the others.

Women did not participate in the village assembly, but they had their own councils from which men were excluded. The nature and influence of the women's councils varied from area to area, but it was not uncommon for them to share responsibility with the village assembly for administering justice. Most men approved of these councils—they believed that women were often more impartial in their judgement. Certainly the spokeswomen were chosen for wisdom, not because of wealth or seniority in the clan.

Women controlled most of the local trade in Iboland. Markets abounded and each village had a specific market day. It was an occasion not simply to buy and sell, but to meet old friends, exchange gossip and hear news of relatives in distant villages. Women thought nothing of spending the greater part of a day trekking to and from a market. Like the village group and marriage ties, markets helped to broaden contacts and maintain peace and stability in the fragmented pattern of village life.

Regional trade strengthened Ibo identity still further. Certain parts of north-eastern Iboland produced a surplus of yams, which were traded to more populous areas in the south. Salt and dried fish were imported from the Niger delta region, cattle and horses from the savannah. Meanwhile, different groups specialized in various crafts and in the provision of ritual and religious services, which led to a great deal of travelling up and down the country. This also stimulated the exchange of information and maintained the wider community of Ibo society.

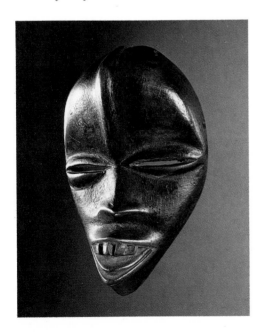

Below: A wooden Dan mask from the Ivory Coast. This is a so-called 'passport' mask to denote acceptance by, or invitation into, a poro secret society. This mask is intended to inspire a certain awe and fear, to protect the secrets of the poro.

A further bond in Ibo society was the system of oracles. Oracles were the mouthpiece for a variety of spirits—nature spirits, locality spirits such as rocks and trees, and ancestral spirits. Some Ibo oracles only had local authority, but four with particularly important and awesome spirits had power throughout the land: the Agballa oracle at Awka, the Igwehe Ala oracle at Umunora, the Amadioha oracle at Ozuzu and the Ibimi Okpabe oracle at Arochuku. These oracles were served by traders, acting as agents, who brought clients from the most distant groups of villages.

The oracles were shrines at which appeals could be made to a god; the resident priest, who acted as mouthpiece, issued the god's verdict after offerings had been made by the client. Ibo oracles acted in many ways; for example, they secured fertility for barren women, guaranteed good harvests and pronounced judgements on disputes. The effectiveness and therefore the fame of an oracle lay in its apparent ability to kill by supernatural means those disobeying its verdict. Generally such supernaturally caused deaths took the form of a lingering illness, which was seen as punishment for disobedience.

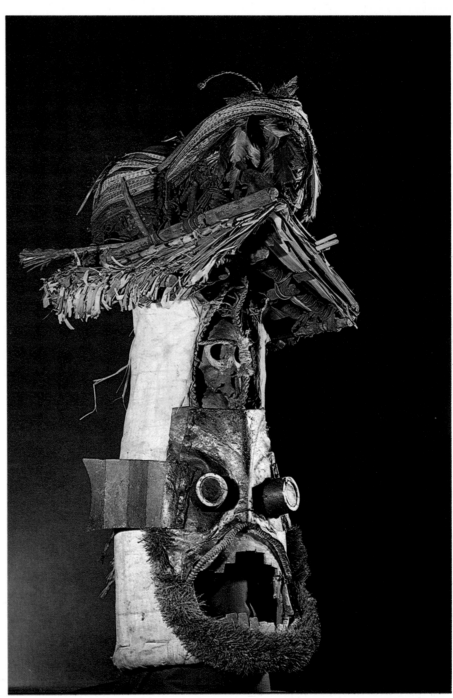

Left : The masks of the forest peoples could be terrifying in the extreme. This Ibibio mask of wood was made for the masquerades of their Ekop secret society. The Ibibio live on the coast of Nigeria, to the east of the Niger delta, and are the neighbours of the Ibo. A society such as the Ekop regularized a host of social, legal, economic and political matters in the absence of a centralized political state. It also gave its members, especially the older members, much social prestige. This is a kind of double mask ; the frightening face of a leper is surmounted by a human skull with the eye sockets pointing skywards.

Right : A headdress from eastern Nigeria used in a dance ceremony. Whereas most West African headdresses are made of wood, this is an accumulative sculpture built up from all kinds of materials. It is a rare object, which expresses different aspects of existence in a seemingly haphazard manner. A monkey's skull sits on top of the actual mask, then there is the roof of a house, astride which lies an animal, possibly a lion.

An oracle would also cause the death of disputants who invoked it falsely. Such offenders were believed to be killed at once, and certainly they were never seen again; witnesses saw trails of blood flowing from the sacred grove of the oracle. What generally happened was that the oracle's priest sacrificed an animal and used its blood, while the victim was hidden and later sold into slavery. However, most litigants were so convinced of a famous oracle's powers that they would be sure to tell the truth.

There is no doubt that the oracles were the single most binding and authoritative force in the basically non-authoritarian Ibo society—significantly it was a religious rather than a political authority. No oracle enjoyed greater prestige than the Ibimi Okpabe oracle at Arochuku. The Aro group of Ibo lived in the east of the country, on the west bank of the Cross river, and their oracle brought them a much greater degree of political unity and economic dynamism than existed elsewhere in the country. It was so widely renowned that even the rulers of the Niger delta city states brought cases for its judgement. By the eighteenth century the Aro had prospered so much from commerce and from the fees their middlemen received for providing safe passage to the oracle that most people did not need to farm to make a living.

Although the Aro monopolized neither trading nor religious interconnections in Iboland, they did play an important role, especially in the eastern districts. Regrettably, they turned to participation in the slave trade. They exploited their links with the other parts of Iboland, and with neighbouring peoples, to become middlemen in a trade in human beings. Slaves from the savannah and plateau areas north of the Benue, and even Ibo who had been captured in raids or forced to become slaves because of economic weakness, were taken to the Aro markets. The Aro were in a position to sell these slaves to whichever coastline slavery state could offer the highest price. They used mercenary troops to raid for more slaves, and to defend the roads and paths, or waterways, down which the slave bands travelled on their way to the coast and eventual transportation to the New World. The Aro monopolized the supply of guns and ammunition to the interior, and so could control a crucial economic and political weapon—by the nineteenth century, they dominated much of Iboland. Yet neither they nor the fearful trade in human beings could destroy the essentially independent and democratic nature of the ancient Ibo way of life.

Different conditions prevailed at the western end of the tropical Guinea rain forest, in present-day Sierra Leone and Liberia. There there lived groups of people such as the Dan, the Temne and the Kru who developed a large degree of cultural homogeneity. Their social organization was in small groups, sometimes tiny areas controlled by petty chiefs, but generally along similar democratic lines to those of the Ibo. They were dependent mainly on hunting, fishing and gathering until early in the Christian era when their eastern neighbours, the Akan, passed on to them the vital trio of Malaysian food-crops: bananas, taros and yams. But it was rice, yet another Malaysian crop, which eventually became the predominant staple of the area. Introduced into West Africa by Berbers and Arabs sometime before 1500, rice was planted first in the Senegal-Gambia region and then in the forest lands further south.

As the coast is so indented, with creeks winding their way deep inland, and numerous fairly small rivers and streams running off the Futa Jallon, fishing remained important to the forest people. However, even in the adverse conditions of the forest most of them kept a few head of cattle mainly for sacrifices or the payment of a bride price. The household unit consisted of an extended family—a man with his wives, children and grandchildren—living in dwellings constructed of mud, wattle, wood and thatch and usually grouped in family compounds. A collection of these compounds formed the small compact village typical of the region, clustered around a central square or open place with a council house.

Isolated in its forest glade, each village was surrounded by a protective

Above : Ibo dance headdress showing a slaver bringing a woman to the slave-trade castles on the Nigerian coast. Note the European hat.

Left : Elmina Castle, Ghana, begun by the Portuguese in 1482, soon after they reached the Gold Coast. It became the headquarters of the Dutch slave-trading activities in 1637, and finally passed into the hands of the British in the nineteenth century. Shown here is a courtyard of the female slave quarters, where the slaves were kept in dungeons at ground level. Directly above were the commander's quarters, conveniently linked by trapdoors to provide access for female slaves to his bedroom. Here the slaves awaited shipment, after procurement from African traders, across the Atlantic to the Americas. Although built under European supervision, Elmina Castle has architectural features in common with indigenous African buildings.

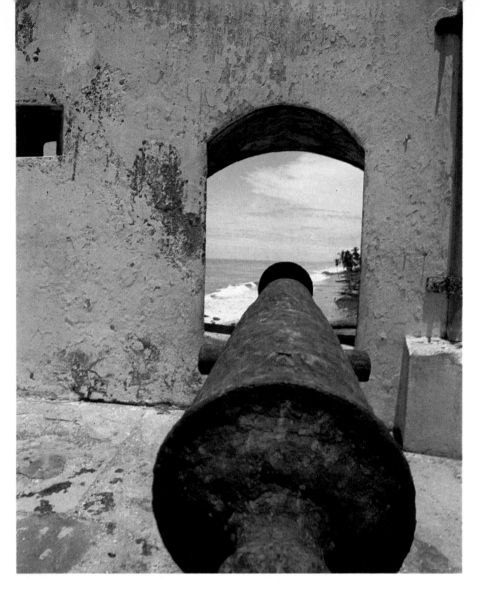

wall or palisade. Trade was not greatly developed, and markets were infrequent. Nevertheless, a unique type of currency, consisting of T-shaped pieces of forged iron, was widespread. Furthermore, the Vai people were one of the only two groups in tropical Africa to create their own system of writing, consisting of a syllabary with 226 characters.

The invasion of two very different groups of newcomers had a crucial effect upon the history of the Western Guinea forests. The first were the Mende, Mande-speaking people from the upper reaches of the Niger and Senegal rivers, who conquered parts of the region in the fifteenth century as part of a larger diaspora of Mande-speaking peoples throughout the western half of West Africa. Fear of the Mende forced the forest peoples to live in stockade villages. The Mende introduced Islam into the forest lands, though not to much effect, and they influenced some of the more powerful local rulers to adopt the style and ritual of the emperor of the great Mali state.

The other invaders were Europeans, whose trading stations on the coast were tiny, but whose slaving activities brought an even greater element of fear and insecurity than the Mende. The first to arrive were the Portuguese, who appeared off the upper Guinea coast in the fifteenth century—about the same time as the first known Mende invasion—and were followed by Dutch, English, French and Americans. Yet despite these pressures, the forest communities expanded. Like the Ibo, these peoples in the Western Guinea forest maintained their democratic structures. But where the Ibo of the eastern forests had their age sets and kinship groups as a bulwark against authoritarianism, African peoples in the western forests were able to resist major changes in the structure of their societies by strengthening the political functions of groups which already enjoyed considerable influence—the secret societies.

Above left : A Portuguese cannon in Elmina Castle, overlooking the surf of the Atlantic. From the end of the fifteenth century, Europeans intruded grimly upon the lives of the coastal people of West Africa. But until the nineteenth century the Europeans remained in their fortresses, where African traders brought slaves from the interior to them. Direct European influence on the great majority of West Africans only occurred after 1800.

Right : This great door was carved by Olowe Ise-Ekiti in eastern Yorubaland about 1915 for the palace of the ogoga or king of the neighbouring town of Ikere-Ekiti. Olowe died in 1939. The carving shows scenes of the ogoga receiving the first British administrator round about 1900. The ogoga appears to be seated on a European-type deck chair, while the administrator, in his sun hat, is being carried in a kind of litter.

Secret societies of a kind existed among the Ibo around the oracles, whose priests formed a clandestine network which operated amongst widely scattered communities to exercise a great deal of political and social control. In Western Guinea their functions and those of Ibo village councils and elders were assumed by distinctly formed societies, whose deliberations were kept secret, but whose membership was open to all male members of the community. Like the looser groupings of Ibo oracle priests, they formed immensely influential networks amongst the diffused peoples in the areas in which they operated.

Among the Mende and Temne peoples the societies were named *poro*, a word meaning 'laws of the ancestors' and which indicates that the power of each poro was given supernaturally by ancestor spirits. The poro controlled the periods of fishing and harvest, regulated trading, and judged disputes in secret tribunals. A large village or small town had its own poro; otherwise there would be one poro in a locality of several villages. The poro was primarily a judicial body, deciding the more intractable intra-village disputes, and all its deliberations were kept strictly secret from the general public. This secretiveness and its supernatural connections gave the poro authority a mystical quality lacking in a Mende chief.

There were also societies which specialized in such activities as military training, ensuring agricultural fertility, curing mental illnesses and enforcing the prohibitions governing sexual relations. In effect, general education, political and economic affairs, sexual conduct and medical and social services were the concern of specific associations. Like the poro, these societies were also secret, in that their deliberations were carried out privately, although the matters on which they decided concerned the whole community.

A counterpart to the all-male poro was provided for women by the *sande* societies which, however, had none of the political power of the poro, but were concerned almost entirely with the initiation of adolescent girls into adult society.

Details of these secret societies varied from people to people, but in general both poro and sande included nearly all adults and provided their members with a general education. Admission to the societies was open to adults and adolescents on payment of a fee and after undergoing initiation rites, and, as membership was so comprehensive, initiation generally meant acceptance into adulthood. Each village in a chiefdom had its own lodge for each society, and boys and girls were initiated at the same time each year. Each group was taken to a sacred place in the forest where the initiation took place. This separation from the family involved not only a cutting-off of lineage ties, but a forging of new bonds with the guardian spirit of the society.

The initiates lived in a miniature world of their own that approximated to life in the larger community, and were given practical training for the future roles of adult men and women. Among the Mende people girls were instructed in homecraft, child care, sexual matters and correct attitudes towards a husband, other men and co-wives. Boys were instructed in the duties of a grown man, including maintaining roads, clearing the bush for farm fields and other agricultural operations; and they were required to provide their own material requirements, including their food.

Boys were also taught crafts, including the making of bridges, traps, nets, basketry and raffia clothes; they practised somersaults and acrobatics; and they learned to drum and sing the poro songs. By means of mock courts and councils in which they enacted the roles of their elders, they were taught traditional laws and customs. They were also expected to bear considerable hardship and suffering without complaint.

The initiation schools turned the boys and girls into men and women able to assume full status in the adult community. Circumcision for the boys and excision for the girls was a painful part of this process; and the boys were symbolically reborn after having been 'eaten' by the poro spirit —cuts were made on their backs to signify the marks of the spirit's teeth.

On page 84 : The West African rain forest. Everything is being burnt for clearance and fertilization from the ash to provide planting areas for food crops. The all-pervasive spirits of the forest who flit amongst the trees have to be pushed back by the fire at the same time.

On page 85 : An Ekoi dance headdress from Nigeria, made of skin and wood. Masks of this sort are used for many masking cults, such as hunters' clubs and age grade societies. This fearsome head probably represents a mythical monkey-man.

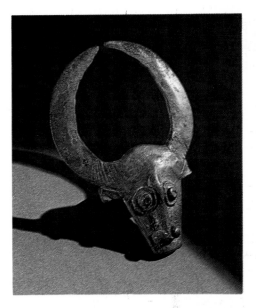

Above : A bronze cast 'ring of silence' from the Senufo people of the Ivory Coast. In certain circumstances, when an initiate had to keep silent, he would put the ring in his mouth.

Left : A wooden Dan mask from the Ivory Coast, used in the ceremony of a poro secret society. The social and religious value of the mask is made explicit by the strings of cowrie shells around the headdress. Cowrie shells were the main currency of much of West Africa.

Both poro and sande spirits appeared as terrifying masked figures, to whom sacrifices were made at the end of the initiations.

The poro had important functions in the government of a chiefdom: only its members could hold political office. Poro was divided into two grades of senior and junior officials and members, with the elders who formed the senior inner council of the society controlling—or strongly influencing—political affairs. This inner council also acted as a judicial authority, and the poro often had the sole right to try important people. It could thus keep a check on an individual's power, for to incur the displeasure of the poro was a rash matter indeed and such delinquents would be smelled out as evil spirits.

A chief could only be influential and wield power if he carried the poro with him. If the senior members of the society in a chiefdom disagreed with the ruler, his authority would not continue to count for much. The poro watched over a dying chief and approved his successor. On the other hand, there were checks to prevent the poro from itself becoming too powerful and totalitarian. There was no central organization of all the lodges; lineages acted with chiefs to check poro influence in local affairs. Ultimately, if the people of a community constantly disapproved of the activities of the poro, their will would prevail.

These secret societies were of very great importance to the peoples of the Western Guinea forests, dominating the lives and livelihoods of several otherwise different peoples. They imparted a sense of comradeship that transcended all barriers of family, clan, ethnic group and religion. Like the institutions of a more centralized state, they established social, political and artistic rules which extended beyond the horizons of the forest villages. They also provided a means of concerted action by many different peoples. In 1898, a great anti-colonial uprising in Sierra Leone began when the poro war sign, a burnt palm leaf, was sent from chief to chief, and village to village—a striking example of the unquestioning allegiance so many owed to it and a vivid demonstration of the way that political leadership could be taken over by the poro. But the main function of the poro was always its mediation between the spirit world and man. Everything to the West African has a spirit, or spirits. Underlying all their activities was the fundamental reality that a poro was a vehicle for this exercise of the spirit powers on the world of man.

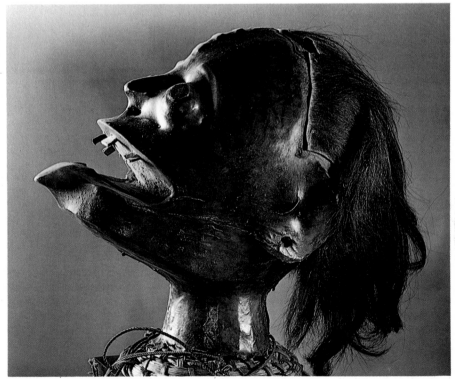

Trade and Crafts

Although my father spoke no word aloud, I knew very well that he was thinking them within. I read it from his lips, which were moving while he bent over the vessel. He kept mixing gold and coal with a wooden stick which would blaze up every now and then and constantly had to be replaced. What could these words be but incantations? Throughout the whole process the Sorcerer's speech became more and more rapid, his rhythms more urgent, and as the ornament took shape, his panegyrics and flatteries increased in vehemence and praised my father's skill to all the heaven . . . the Sorcerer did in truth take part in the work. He too was drunk with the joys of creation and loudly proclaimed his joy; enthusiastically he snatched the strings, became inflamed, as if he himself were the craftsman, as if he himself were my father, as if the ornament were coming from his own hands.

(C. Laye *African Child* London 1955)

Left : The river harbour at Mopti in Mali. The middle Niger and all its tributaries was the great waterway and main commercial artery of much of the western Sudan, and towns such as Mopti, Timbuktu, Gao and Jenné were not only centres of trade and industry, but also of administration and learning. The two great medieval Muslim Sudanic empires, Mali and Songhay, had their core around this huge stretch of inland waterway. River cities such as Mopti attracted commerce from all over the savannah lands to the south and from Mediterranean Africa across the Sahara to the north. Goods were transferred from donkeys and camels onto large canoes, to be shipped up or down the Niger.

The spectacular variety of social forms and customs in West Africa was influenced to some extent by the different ecological conditions in which people lived. Of the great centralized empires, for example, only Benin developed entirely within the forest—all the others were formed on the savannah, where the ground was better suited to cavalry warfare and thus to political control over large areas. Elsewhere, and particularly in the forests, states and kingdoms were on a smaller scale. Furthermore, since most West Africans lived by agriculture, they formed static, settled communities and rarely travelled far beyond the village. Turning inwards, they evolved customs peculiar to themselves, only occasionally influenced by the outside world.

However, that ideas did spread through the area testifies to two conditions. First, people migrated and took their knowledge from one region to another. But also, as the principle of producing an agricultural surplus became widely established, information was diffused by traders and other travellers, substantial trading networks grew up and only the most isolated villages remained outside them. In particular the traders came for gold which was exchanged for salt. Gold was the main trade item until the development of slavery in the seventeenth century.

Like the ripples formed when a pebble is thrown into a pond, traders spread out in ever-increasing circles from many different bases. First there was the exchange of local produce, often through a series of near-by markets. Then, fanning out from these, taking produce from them and bringing back specialized goods, was a host of middle-distance networks.

Finally came international trade, which was concerned only with a handful of commodities but was organized over vast distances and linked West Africa with Europe and the Arab world.

William Bosman, who worked for the Dutch West India Company in the early years of the eighteenth century, left an account of how one coastal community responded to small-scale trade with particular enthusiasm:

> 'Besides Agriculture, from which the King and a few great Men are only exempted, their Manufactures are spinning of Cotton, weaving of fine Cloaths, making of Calabasses, wooden Vessels, Assagayes and Smiths-ware; and several other Handicrafts . . . Whilst the Men are so diligently employed, the Women are not idle; they brew, or rather boil Beer, and dress Victuals, which they carry to Market to sell together with their Husband's Merchandize: So that both Men and Women here are employed in getting of Money, and each zealously strives to outdo the other.' (William Bosman *A New and Accurate Description of the Coast of Guinea* London 1705)

Quite distinct groups of people came to monopolize the different types of trade. By and large, international trade was operated by foreigners—Berbers and Arabs in the north, Europeans in the south. Over the centuries regional trade, however, became the speciality, most notably, of the Mande-speaking Dyula in the west and the Hausa further east. While the Dyula had no established trading centres of their own, the Hausa, on the other hand, operated from a string of powerful city states in the north of what is now Nigeria. Like many other political developments in the Sudan, these Hausa cities were originally founded by people moving southwards from the desert—in this case. Negro agriculturalists from the Air Mountains. Competition for the land best provided with subterranean water resulted in a number of densely populated agricultural communities emerging in areas which were quite northerly by West African standards.

The Hausa rulers, or *sarkin*, lived in walled towns, among the most famous of which were Kano, Katsina, Zaria and Gobir. Together with a wealthy aristocracy, the sarkin owned land in the neighbouring countryside, which was cultivated by peasants living outside the cities. It was only in the fifteenth or sixteenth centuries that they began to engage in trade, sending luxury goods and gold across the Sahara. Within the cities Hausa craftsmen manufactured such luxury goods as very fine leatherwork, while other Hausa travelled far and wide to Asante, Yorubaland and Benin, selling weapons, armour and horses, and buying gold, cloth and kola nuts.

Kola trees grew throughout the forest regions, but were especially prolific in Asante. The nut's twin interlocking kernels were regarded as a symbol of friendship; no present was complete without kola, and it became customary to swear oaths on a kola nut. A mildly addictive stimulant with a pleasantly bitter flavour, kola is very sustaining in hot, dry climates and is widely regarded as a cure for impotence. As one of the few stimulants allowed by Islam, it was well worth carrying across the Sahara to the Muslim lands to the north, although the heavy cost of transport from the forest plantations made it a luxury item. It was carefully placed in bags covered by wet leaves which kept the fruit fresh.

Salaga, to the north of Asante, was one of the great Hausa trading centres in the nineteenth century, and a base for the kola trade. The German traveller Henry Barth left an account of its operations:

> 'Three points are considered essential to the business of the kola trade: first, that the people of Mossi bring their asses; secondly, that the natives of Asante bring the nut in sufficient quantities; and thirdly, that the state of the road is such as not to prevent the Hausa people from arriving. The price of the asses rises with the cheapness of the kola. The average price of an ass in the market of Salaga is 15,000 [cowrie] shells; while in Hausa the general price does not

exceed 5,000. But the *tatahi*, or native traders, take only as many asses with them from Hausa as are necessary for transporting their luggage, as the toll, or *titto*, levied upon each ass by the petty chiefs on the road is very considerable.' (H. Barth *Travels and Discoveries in North and Central Africa* vol II, London and New York 1965)

Strong trading ties often developed between the kola nut and gold, and this brought the Hausa into competition with other traders at the Asante gold fields. The Dyula, in particular, had begun to specialize in long-distance trade well before the Hausa, moving away from their homelands in small family groups but keeping close kinship ties which connected individuals across vast distances. Although basically agriculturalist they found niches in other societies by performing their services as traders.

Like other Mande-speakers, they were converted early to Islam, and indeed played a major role in taking the religion to other West Africans. An English merchant called Robert Jobson, who encountered the Dyula traders on the Gambia river in 1620, actually described them as 'Mary-bucks', from the Arabic term *marabout*, or holy man:

'They goe in companies together, and drive before them their Asses, whose ordinary pace they follow, beginning the dayes journey, when the day appears, which is even at the Sunne rising and continue travelling some three houres, then they are enforced to rest all the heate of the day, some two houres before the Sunne setteth, going forward againe, and so continue untill night comes, whenas they are sure to harbour themselves, for feare of wilde beastes, except in some shadie trees, close to the town, set forth such things as they have to sale, maintaining in the time they are there a kind of market.' (R. Jobson, quoted in Bovell *The Golden Trade* London 1932)

The Dyula specialized in the gold trade from its earliest days. One of the most extraordinary features of the remarkable international trading complex that developed was that the source of the gold of West Africa, which

was after all the reason for the whole dangerous undertaking, was a well-kept secret. Arab merchants certainly did not know where it was mined. It was obvious to them that the rulers of the great West African empire were wealthy in gold, but the actual source remained a mystery. The gold in fact originated to the west and to the south, the main field being in Buré, south of the Mali empire, and was transported to the southern entrepôts of the Saharan trade routes by the Dyula. But even they did not come into direct contact with the producers of the precious metal. The miners kept the secrets of their craft so closely guarded that even imperial officers were refused access to their lands. When the Mali authorities tried to take over Buré, the miners simply went out on strike; they stopped production. Even when the moment of the transaction came the miners did not come into face-to-face contact with the traders, but used the system of 'dumb-barter' (as in the description by Herodotus at the beginning of the second chapter).

Yet the Mende, known as *Wangara* to the Arabs, gradually achieved a special relationship with their trading partners. Valentin Fernandez, an early European traveller to the area, wrote of them in the sixteenth century:

'The traders belong to a particular race, called the Ungaros [Wangara]; they are red or brownish. In fact, only the members of this race, to the exclusion of others, are allowed to approach the mines, because they are considered trustworthy. No other person, whether white or black, can get there. When these Ungaros arrive at Jenné, each trader brings along with him one or two hundred black slaves, or even more, to carry the salt on their heads from Jenné to the gold mines, and to bring back gold . . . They trust each other without receipts, written agreements, or witnesses. The credit that they are given extends until a certain date in the year, because the Ungaros come to Jenné once a year only. They are so honest that if one of them died before the payment was due, his son or his heir would hastily repay the debt exactly.' (V. Fernandez *Description de la côte d'Afrique de Ceuta au Sénégal* Paris 1938)

Above: A Yoruba bowl called an 'ajere ifa'. Bowls such as this could have been used as containers for kola nuts, the only stimulant allowed by strict Muslims, but were also important in divination.

Left : A brass container with lid, made by Akan people, Asante. This kind of container was known as 'kuduo', and was used for gold dust and valuables. It was sometimes buried with its owner. The country of the Akan was one of the richest sources of gold in West Africa. Much of this was transported across the Sahara, either in containers such as this one, or as ingots, to the Muslim lands of the Middle East or to Christian Europe, where it formed the basis of the gold currency of the states of these areas.

Right : A Tuareg silversmith at work in his tent in the Air region of northern Nigeria. He is still nomadic, and has three wives. This kind of small forge was commonly used by smiths throughout West Africa at one time.

No contemporary accounts have survived to record how the gold was mined, although it is known that some gold was washed out of the rivers and streams flowing off the low ranges of hills around Buré. However, the method was probably the same as the one being followed by the Asante as recently as 1960, when gold was still being produced from a system of parallel rows of holes about 75 centimetres (2 ft 6 ins.) in diameter and about 12 metres (40 ft) deep. Underground, the miners joined up the shafts with a grid of tunnels about one metre (3 ft) high, and removed the soft, gold-bearing alluvium with a short-handled pick. At this depth there was water in the tunnels, so the pay dirt was placed in large calabashes and floated back to the shafts for preliminary washing. It was then hauled to the surface, where women carried out a second wash in pools of water close by. The miners, their wives and daughters who washed the alluvium, a smith who maintained the picks and a director of operations who also sold the gold, formed a fairly stable and balanced team.

Goldminers were traditionally feared because they had access to the magic beneath the earth's surface. Craftsmen were generally accorded a special status in West African society, depending upon the particular craft they practised. Blacksmiths, above all, were set apart. Like the traders, both they and the goldminers achieved a special position in society, but suffered a kind of ostracism because their secret knowledge was considered dangerous and disruptive. In many parts of West Africa blacksmiths were kept so much apart from the ordinary people that they formed a distinct caste, with their own initiation rites.

Among the hill people of middle Nigeria, most little kingdoms had four major hereditary social groupings: a ruling clan, commoners, bond servants, and finally blacksmiths. The men of this caste were also the undertakers and produced the leatherworks—thus most of the rulers' clothes—for the kingdom, while the women were the society's potters and helped their husbands with the leathercraft. In many instances blacksmiths were even diviners and medicine-men, and performed other specialized tasks.

They were not regarded as true members of the society by the majority, nor could they move into the other classes. Blacksmiths and other citizens never ate or drank together, yet the distinction was one neither of inferiority nor superiority. The origin myths of these kingdoms even suggest ties between the blacksmiths and the royal clan. The founding ancestor of one kingdom was befriended by blacksmiths and, using their arrows, killed both his enemies and much game. When he shared his kill of game with his neighbours, they were so impressed with his generosity and skill that they made him their leader. In another instance a founding ancestor was given an old female member of the blacksmith caste to cook for him. When she conceived, the father was recognized as having unusual powers and was made their leader.

These stories were used to explain why many kings of the hill people were required to marry a female member of the blacksmith caste, in apparent violation of the marital prohibition. In all the ceremonies relating to the kings, the blacksmiths played a prominent part.

Iron itself also featured prominently in West African origin myths and was associated with particular gods and cults. It was the most important metal for daily affairs, and so, of all the craftsmen it was probably the blacksmith who was the most highly valued. The farmer depended on him to make and maintain his tools; the soldier and the hunter turned to him for their weapons. And the smith was also called upon to make ritual objects and figures for use in religious and initiation ceremonies. He needed great skill and authority to imbue his work with the power that religious paraphernalia had to possess in order to be effective. Thus the smith became an intermediary between man and the spirit world.

The Dogon especially accorded the blacksmith a unique position. They have one particular myth which tells how man first began to work and dance. At the beginning of the world there were eight spirits who were formless creatures with fluid, jointless limbs—life-giving water was their essence. The seventh spirit was the blacksmith, who stole a piece of the sun in the form of live coals and incandescent iron and escaped down the rainbow with his prize. The blacksmith's impact when landing on earth was so violent that the hammer and anvil he was carrying smashed his jointless limbs, thus creating knees and elbows which allow men to work and dance. The Dogon also believe that the blacksmith was responsible for bringing man's earliest ancestors to earth, as well as animals, seeds and the beginnings of technology.

Dogon blacksmiths sometimes became wood-carvers, and were commissioned to produce a variety of objects. Large carved figures were often the home of the spirit of family ancestors; they were also protective, a guarantee of fertility and long life. Large or small carvings representing family ancestors were often more naturalistic than carvings of the earliest ancestors, but the carver was concerned above all with the essence of the object carved. He wanted to recreate it as the deity had designed it at the beginning of the world.

The blacksmith or professional wood-carver did not usually make masks, which had a different function from carved figures and had a greater secrecy attached to them. These were usually carved by young men during their initiation into manhood, following the guidance of their elders. The masks sometimes represented animals, ranging from antelope and monkey to crocodile and rhinoceros. Others represented the priest—the *hogon*—or a hunter.

The Great Masks, however, could only be carved by initiated members of the mask cult, and were rarely worn. Up to 9 metres (30 ft) in height, they were carved from a single piece of wood taken from a particular kind of tree, and were associated with the Legendary Ancestor. According to Dogon tradition the first Great Mask was carved when death came into the world. Before death was known, family elders simply turned into serpents or tree-like beings, but when the cult secrets were betrayed to a non-initiate all men were punished by being made mortal. The community

Left : A Dogon dancing figure made of iron. This remarkable dancer is typical of the grace, simplicity and reductionism of much of Dogon art. There is a great sense of movement here, of liberation. The objects attached to the arms, foot and head are clappers.

then faced a threat from the power released when an individual died, and two masks were carved to meet this crisis. One, the Great Mask, represented a serpent; the other was an old man. Together they enabled the Dogon to absorb the spirits of dead men.

Masks were often closely associated with a secret cult and the carvers of masks were invariably leading members of the society surrounding the cult. The wood-carvers of the Senufo, who live in the northern part of the Ivory Coast, belonged to a caste known as Kule and usually lived together in a particular quarter of their town or village. They were members of the poro, whose leader wore a 'devil' mask during the initiation and burial rituals.

When the masks were not in use, they were hidden from sight in a sacred grove. The skill of the carvers and the rituals which they had performed had endowed the masks with life and power which could not be allowed to seep away. Wood-carvers were regarded as vital to the well-being of the community, for without them there could be no masks to contain and tap the power of the spirits. Yet all societies valued other craftsmen, too—for example, dyers of cloth, spinners and weavers, potters, leather-workers and musicians.

Spinners and weavers were rarely accorded the special status of the more specialized craftsmen. Yet they were essential to the community, and myths, rituals and taboos grew up around them. The Bambara and the Dogon associate the process of spinning and weaving with man's advancement from his primitive state before death came into the world. At that time man was naked and had no knowledge of speech. They relate how the Supreme God gave man weaving and speech to help him develop his culture. Bambara mythology claims that it was the spider spinning its web which first gave man the idea of weaving:

'The spider wove its web across a corner of the doorway of a young Bambara man, Diara Dara, who noticed the work in progress and with his friend, Kari Mariko, sought to imitate the spider. First they used the fine threads of the spider, but, failing, they moved to try the threads of cotton spun by their wives. In a rudimentary fashion, they wove the first *cache-sexe*.

To aid in passing the weft through the warp, Kari Mariko constructed the first shuttle . . . The process of weaving was revealed to man, and immediately labelled a male domain. It is an act of the day, and the looms of the Bambara are set out in the sunlight. A pot is pierced and buried in the ground beneath the spot chosen for sitting. In this act allusion is made to the impregnating of woman by man and the entering of the warp by the weft.' (D. Fraser ed. *African Art as Philosophy* New York 1974)

This association between weaving and sexual intercourse is quite common, and the taboos and rituals integral to the art often have their origins in this analogy. A Dogon man can weave by day, but if he weaves at night, when he should be with his wife, he may go blind. Weaving in most societies is a man's work, while the less skilled job of spinning the cotton falls to women. The Asante have never allowed a woman to weave because she menstruates—a menstruating woman is regarded as a threat to the community because she is temporarily infertile. The wife of an Asante weaver was not allowed even to touch the loom or speak directly to her husband while she was menstruating.

Other non-sexual taboos accrued to weaving. It was forbidden for an Asante weaver to break up or burn his loom. The accidental breaking of a loom was considered a bad omen and the weaver had to sacrifice a fowl over it. If he was to undertake a long journey or spend several months away trading he would throw the parts of his loom into the river to ensure that it could never be broken up for firewood.

Most Asante weavers produced cloth which would be worn by ordinary

Right: Nana Amonu X, Omanhene of Anomabu, a Fante chief from Ghana. The Akan people from Fanteland and Asante were renowned weavers and dyers of cloth. The pattern of the cloth of the chief's robes is often reserved for him and may not be used on cloth for other people.

Left : A bronze relief from Benin, made
about 1600. Here the drummers in court
dress are performing at one of the state
ceremonies of the oba's court in Benin City.

Right : A horn player from Benin. Music
accompanied nearly all ceremonies in West
Africa, from the most pompous court
rituals of the great kings and emperors to the
dances and recreations of humble villagers.

people, but the most skilled were chosen to weave beautiful patterned cloth
for the asantehene and important chiefs. All new designs used in weaving
were held to be the copyright of the asantehene. Each pattern had a name
and sometimes a meaning: one was called *adweneasa*, meaning 'my skill is
exhausted' or 'my ideas have come to an end'. It was a highly complex and
intricate pattern and only the master weavers could produce it. The order
to weave this pattern was the prerogative of the king.

In many societies, the craft groups employed musicians to entertain and
inspire them. In Hausaland the blacksmiths, butchers, praise singers, and
even farmers, had musicians each with their own particular instruments,
especially drums. There were also musicians for the religious groups,
some belonging to the strict Muslim mosques and schools, others to the
wilder pagan cults, or *bori*. At cult ceremonies, the drumming produced a
heightened emotional state in the singing and dancing which was basic to
a bori performance. Indeed, the most important bori spirit was called the
'chief of the drummers', and the musicians consulted this spirit when they
had professional difficulties.

There were musicians for recreation—dances for children and young
people, sexually inspired dances, music in the houses of prostitutes and in
drinking places. Other musicians were attached permanently to the royal
courts; indeed, these were so numerous that they formed court bands.

Training systems for novice craftsmen varied between the different
societies, but all shared the view that the craftsmen depended closely on the
spirit world. This is shown by the way Yoruba children were taught craft
skills, which was either by their parents, or through apprenticeship.
Whether a boy learnt quickly or slowly, and whether he became a successful
carver or a poor one, was explained by the Yoruba in terms of the personal
destiny assigned to him at birth by the Sky God Olorun. If an apprentice
could do better work than his teacher, people knew that the skill was given
to him by Olorun as part of his destiny, which included the occupation
that he was to follow. Soon after a child was born, the parents consulted a
diviner to learn its destiny, and an individual might have to sacrifice to
Olorun at various times during his life, when instructed by the diviners.

If a Yoruba boy was apprenticed to a master craftsman, it was usually
for a specific period and a fixed fee. Some lived with and were fed by their
masters; others returned home for their evening meals and lodging. The
apprentice served as his master's assistant, running errands and performing

Above: A Janus-type headdress made by the Idoma of Nigeria, who are neighbours of the Yoruba. We see a female face painted on wood, with human hair. The other side is a male, of which only the goatee beard is visible here.

other odd tasks for him. Beginning with simple techniques and simple objects, he carved or wove under the direction of his teacher until he had mastered his craft. The master provided the necessary materials and owned whatever the apprentice produced—in some cases the boy even had to give his master part of his earnings after the period of apprenticeship had ended.

In almost every aspect of 'artistic' expression in West Africa—sculpting, carving, weaving, smelting, musicianship, dancing—no distinction was made between the work of the artist, craftsman or performer and that of the religious life and experience of his society. In effect, he operated as the very core of his people's experience.

As in most pre-literate communities, it was through craftsmen that knowledge of the past was handed down from generation to generation. In many cases, this process was deliberately controlled by the rulers. The tailors and *appliqué* workers of Dahomey, for instance, became the official craftsman-historians of the kingdom; producing richly-coloured tents, ceremonial umbrellas and tapestries, at first embroidered and later in appliqué. Hung on the walls of the royal palace, or paraded during ceremonial occasions, they told the history of Dahomey.

The kings were represented by special symbols and every Dahomean citizen would be familiar with each king's symbol. King Agaja, who ruled at the beginning of the eighteenth century, was responsible for expanding the frontiers south to the Atlantic coast. Thus, his symbol is a ship. King Gezo consolidated the work begun by Agaja and is probably the most revered of all Dahomey's kings. A brilliant warrior and a skilled politician, his strength is represented by a buffalo. When Gezo died his son, Gelele, succeeded him. He could not match the achievements of his father but he was much feared as a warrior, and is accordingly symbolized by a lion.

The themes of the *appliqué* work evoked the heroism of a king and the important events of his reign. It was a subtle way of enhancing his authority and prestige. Since history was the monopoly of the royal dynasty, the craftsmen produced work which glorified the sovereign. Similarly, in Benin the most skilled craftsmen were chosen to work exclusively for the Oba. Unlike the ordinary craftsmen who carved in wood, the royal master-craftsmen worked with more precious materials: bronze, copper, ivory and coral. The bronze-casters could be put to death if they were commissioned to work for anyone else.

How the craftsmen of Benin first learned bronze-casting is not known for certain, but stylistic similarities between the early Benin bronzes and the beautiful brass heads produced in Ife suggest that the technique came from there. A Benin legend confirms that at the start of the fifteenth century 'Oba Ogula wished to introduce brass casting into Benin so as to produce works of art similar to those sent him from Ife. He therefore sent to the Oni of Ife for a brass-smith and Iguegha was sent to him. Iguegha was very clever and left many designs to his successors, and was in consequence deified and is worshipped to this day by brass-smiths' (J. Egharevba *A Short History of Benin* Ibadan 1960).

The craftsmen of Benin have never lost their knowledge of the casting technique, but those of Ife have produced no bronze or brass figures for several hundred years. Ife traditions suggest an answer as to why this highly prized skill should so mysteriously have been lost. One of the onis of Ife died, but his followers determined to keep his death a secret. Perhaps he had been a much-loved leader or perhaps they feared a terrible struggle for succession would follow his death. They commanded the bronze-casters of the oni to make a portrait-figure of him which was so life-like that everyone would believe that the oni still lived. The bronze-casters did their work so well that they brought about their own doom. The new oni was enraged at what they had done and he ordered that all the artists should be killed. When they died the art of bronze-casting died with them.

Like those of Ife, the master-craftsmen of Benin used their skills to

Right : A brass head from Ife, Yorubaland, Nigeria, made probably in the fourteenth century. This, and other Ife brass heads, are among the masterpieces of African, and indeed of world, sculpture.

Below: A fine example of bronze-casting from Benin, made about 1600. A mudfish-legged oba is supported by two courtiers. Mudfish abound in the creeks and streams of the forests of Benin, and one legend relates the origin of the Edo people to this unprepossessing animal. Certainly the early Edo, before the rise of the great kingdom, made their living chiefly from fishing. It is more likely that this particular oba was deformed, and was depicted as mudfish-legged to hide this fact, since any kind of physical deformity would have debarred him from office.

celebrate the king, and evolved a style which was used only for royal works of art. The oba's palace was decorated with delicately carved ivory, sculpted figures and heads, and plaques cast in bronze. The wall plaques showed in relief scenes illustrating life in the Benin court and in the bustling city of Benin itself. Merchants, Portuguese soldiers and traders are shown, as well as court musicians, hunters, warriors, animals and birds. But the central figure in most of the plaques is the oba. He dominates the scene, all-powerful and semi-divine.

The oba is frequently shown as a fish-legged figure, supported on either side by two of his retainers. The Benin people sometimes argue that this figure is in fact Olokun, god of the sea, fertility and wealth. His affinity with water and the sea is symbolized by the mudfish feet. However, it seems likely that the figure represents an oba who was deformed, for a famous court historian tells of an Oba Ohen who became paralysed after he had reigned for more than twenty years. Since the well-being and safety of the people depended on the strength and good health of the ruler, Oba Ohen would almost certainly have been killed if his paralysis had become known. As he found it increasingly difficult to hide his deformity he told the chiefs and the people that the god Olokun had possessed him and that his legs, like those of Olokun, were sacred and should be hidden away. Perhaps he commanded his brass-smiths to transform his deformity and show him in the plaques as a mysterious and god-like creature.

The copper used in making bronze was a highly valued metal, imported either across the Sahara or, after the sixteenth century, from Europe. But bronze alone could not protect Benin from collapse. The empire began to decline during the seventeenth century and this was reflected in the art. The delicate and sensitive work of the ivory carvings and the bronze plaques gave way to work which was coarser and more stylized. The power of the oba was slipping away and the pressure on the craftsmen to enhance his authority in works of art must have increased. Even at the height of the empire, the bronze-casters had been the servants of their masters, but a certain freedom born of confidence had now been lost for ever.

In most states, the master-craftsmen who worked exclusively for the king settled in or around the palace and were often organized into societies or guilds. They served to promote the king's authority not only by interpreting history, but also through the creation of regalia sceptres, staffs of office or carved stools. Many of these objects were made of precious metals such as gold and silver, so workers of these materials became among the most respected of craftsmen.

Regalia were equally important for the expansion and diffusion of authority. The Asante rulers made gifts of state umbrellas, carved stools and drums, fine woven cloth or gold-handled swords to the heads of lesser states they had conquered or who had become their allies. They wanted these states to be integrated into the Asante Federation, not simply in a political and economic sense, but also culturally, deeming military power alone was not sufficient to build a greater, united Asante.

The most important symbol of all was the Golden Stool, which was thought to contain the soul of the Asante nation. As chiefs and the heads of important families had their own carved stools, in which the souls of a man's ancestors were believed to reside, the creation of a stool was highly important and the craftsman had to approach his work with great care.

The carver had to take the wood from a particular kind of tree. The Asante believed that all trees and plants have spirits, and that some of them have power to do evil. There were three different types of trees which could be used in carving and each had a potentially vindictive spirit. Before he cut the tree down the wood-carver would make an offering to appease the spirit of the tree. He might break an egg over it and make the following plea: 'I am coming to cut you down and carve you, receive this egg and eat . . . do not let the iron cut me; do not let me suffer in health.'

Cutting down the tree released the spirit and left it homeless and disembodied, a potential source of evil. So when he had finished the stool, the carver had to persuade the tree spirit to return to its old home. It was lured back, summoned by a drum call, and rites would be performed—an egg broken over the stool or a fowl sacrificed—to encourage the spirit and sanctify the new carving.

Most of the Asante wood-carvers did not work simply for a king or chief. Much of their carving was for rites; they carved to please the gods. The people of Asante saw the wood-carvers as a link between the gods and spirits and men: thus they were called the spokesmen of the gods.

Religion and craft were indivisible, as much for the common people and their political leaders as for the craftsmen. They sought to capture the vital forces of life in their work, to become themselves instruments of the spirits. Although the skills of individual craftsmen were recognized and valued, their products were not designed to express a single personality or attitude. Their achievements were the achievements of the community, their art imbued with magic.

Art, Priests and the Spirit World

The stream crosses the path,
The path crosses the stream;
Which of them is the elder?
Did we not cut a path long ago to go and meet
*   this stream?*
The stream had its origin long, long ago
The stream had its origin in the Creator,
He created things,
Pure, pure Tano.

(Anon., quoted in E. G. Parrinder *African Traditional Religion* London 1974, New York 1976)

Above : A cast brass Ife figure discovered at the Nupe village of Tada on the middle course of the Niger river in Nigeria. It is almost life-size.

Left : The head of the above figure. The quiet repose, the feeling that the features are looking inwards, are indicative of human suffering accepted with grace and courage.

The art of West African peoples was, primarily, magico-religious in character, and was founded on beliefs about life and death, about heaven and hell, about life-in-death. Sculpture, bas-reliefs, carvings, metalwork, music, dance—all served a specific and often functional end; and their creation was guided by rules belonging to the world of magic.

Art was not conceived in terms of beauty or other aesthetic notions; indeed, West African languages lacked a word for 'beauty' or 'beautiful'. The closest to such a concept are words meaning 'good', 'harmonious', or a term such as 'that from which nothing is lacking'. Art was valued not for art's sake, not as an end in itself, but as possessing an integrative function, making man, and his environment, whole. In West Africa, participation in art bound individuals into communion with their family, clan, tribe or nation, and involved them on a rarefied, 'extra-sensory' plane in the drama of creation. This form of magic was at the core of most African cultures.

The object, the work of art, was the bearer of the forces of life. Although the concept exists throughout the region, there is no single or useful West African word for these forces, so we will use the Bantu word for them, *nyama* (the Bantu-speaking peoples live south of the Equator). The artist, the sculptor, the maker of masks, was a person who could make contact with the nyama by the proper construction and use of artefacts. He was, naturally, considered to be a magician or a witch and his work consisted of a series of ritual acts, from the assembly of the basic materials to the consecration of the object. These acts were often performed in a highly charged emotional state, 'a sacred fire' induced by means of magic.

Above : This wooden staff comes from Yoruba country in south-western Nigeria. It is an oshe sango staff, representing the god of thunder and lightning. It was carved by a sango priest and used in religious ceremonies, sometimes to prevent violent tropical rainstorms. Lying mainly in the tropical forest belt, Yorubaland had, if anything, too much rain. In the north official rainmakers ensured good rains. Sango is always recognizable by the double axe-shaped headdress.

The plastic forms of the art itself were partly dictated by the conventions or traditions of the community, but were essentially the result of what the psyche of the producer or artist had 'seen' in states of ecstasy. The style of the end-product was the record of a particular people's vision of supra-sensible reality. The artist 'saw' with the eyes of the group to which he belonged: his vision was the vision of his people.

West Africans worshipped many different gods. For example, the Asante had a high regard for their nature gods, especially those associated with water, the life-giving force. The most important was the god of the river Tano, and the tributaries of this river were said to be his wives and children. The Yoruba also recognized the spiritual power of nature. Sango was the god of thunder (and of war) and several of his wives were river goddesses. His favourite wife was Oya, goddess of the river Niger, believed to be the power behind the wind which always precedes a thunderstorm.

But behind this polytheism was a recognition that these gods were lesser deities, intermediaries between mankind and the Supreme Being. God's attitude to his creation was held generally to be one of indifference: he was seldom thought to require worship, or a cult devoted especially to him. God was held to be everywhere: he permeated the entire world. If, however, he did have any contact with the men he had created, it was with the group, not with the individual.

If an individual ever sought to make contact with God, it was on the rare and crucial occasions of life: birth, initiation, marriage and death. Even then, the contact made was collective, not individual. Everyday worship was of ancestral spirits and the spirits of other natural forces more readily accessible and tangible than the godhead. The very closeness of these forces to the earth, their material aspects, meant that they were more likely to be affected by men's actions, good or bad.

Having created the world (or, as the Yoruba believe, having delegated this responsibility to one of the lesser gods), the Supreme Being had removed himself to a far corner of the sky. One Asante myth places the blame for this on an old woman who pounded her yams and cassava near the home of the Supreme Being. He then lived in the sky just above the earth. The old woman's pestle was too long and kept striking the Supreme Being. He became very angry and finally resolved to move far away, where mankind could no longer reach him.

To West Africans, invisible forces were no less real than the objects of everyday life; the vivid world of magic was their response to the all-powerful natural forces which formed their environment. Material reality and spirit were not separate existences. On the contrary, everything was felt to be in a state of cohesion, as if the cosmos were a sea of fluid forces perpetually vibrating and manifesting themselves in different ways in particular times and places. Ancestor worship—the rites aimed at establishing and maintaining communion with the founders of the tribe—was a purely terrestrial concept. There was no notion of spirits inhabiting a separate heaven or paradise. The ancestors were part of the material order of this world and, though invisible, were still subject to some at least of its physical laws. They even required nourishment, and food offerings formed an important part of burial ceremonies. In this totality the mental tension in an individual between 'the World and I' was the product of many voices. All the members of the group—family, lineage, clan and tribe—were fused into a single unit not only with each other, but with their ancestors as well.

When someone died, sometimes a fetish or 'double' of the dead person was made in the form of a statuette, using ritual techniques evolved by the witch-doctor or priest. They charged the statue with vital life-energy to enable it to establish contact with other levels of existence.

Integral to this religious world view was the idea of fertility in its many forms, the principle notion being that all organic life on earth, including humanity, had its place in a cosmic economy. It was therefore necessary to exalt the vital energy, the nyama, on which the cosmos was nourished, in

Right : A water spirit mask, used in dance ceremonials. This wooden mask comes from the Ijo in the dense forests and mangrove swamps on the western side of the Niger delta. The small faces carved on it represent the spirit's children—possibly the smaller streams and creeks that provided a livelihood for these fishermen. The dance ceremony would invoke the spirit's goodwill towards the Ijo.

all the forms and shapes in which it is found. This idea moulded social institutions, rites, individual lives and artistic products, and in sculpting human figures particular emphasis was placed on the genital organs. Sex and procreation were the essence of the West African cosmos, and this was nowhere better expressed than in dance.

The fusion of religion and sexuality is a motivating principle in dance, perhaps the crucial, and the most vital, medium of popular culture throughout the region. It was acutely physical, involving the whole person; it was also deeply emotional, conveying hopes and fears, joy and grief, and basic sexual urges. West Africans danced for many reasons and on many occasions; they danced for fun and for the very joy of existence; they danced ironically, to mock or to mimic (and thereby render harmless) neighbouring and potentially dangerous peoples and spirits. Dance provided the public recognition of seasonal or environmental change, of times of sowing and of harvesting; and of crises in the human life-cycle, of birth, puberty and initiation, of marriage, of the passing from warrior to elder, and of death. Dance legitimized political events—there were war dances on the eve of campaigns and after victories, dances at the accession of a new chief, king or emperor, and dances at the funeral of an old one. Above all, dance was profoundly religious: one of the principle links between man and his ancestors, and the gods and spirits of his world.

Masks were always prominent in the religious aspects of dance. Many

Left : Painted cloth used for the costumes of wild animal and fire-spitter masqueraders from the Senufo of the Ivory Coast. The painting represents a dancer wearing a fire-spitter mask surrounded by turtles, lizards and other magic symbols. Fire-spitter was the name given by Europeans who saw the ceremony, held at dusk, in which coals and sparks came out of the mouth of the mask.

Right : This remarkable wooden carving is a marionette used by the Bambara of Mali. The antelope is a representation of the mythical hero (half-antelope, half-man) who taught the Bambara their agricultural skills. It is associated with fertility rites, as distinct from merely recreational performances, and shows most arrestingly the cycle of generational reappearance of the same being with both common and individual characteristics.

Left : A huge Toma mask representing a mythical bird. The Toma are one of the Mende people of Liberia and Guinea.

Right : A wooden dance headdress made by the Afo, who are akin to the Yoruba. The animal gingerly creeping over the knife-like spikes is a chameleon.

peoples of West Africa had mask societies, of which the poro are examples, some of which performed openly and in public, while others were veiled in the greatest secrecy. Very commonly membership of masked societies was restricted to one sex: the Plateau peoples of Jos in modern Nigeria completely forbade their womenfolk to see the masks used by the men, and in more recent times, the women of these tribes have taken great delight in seeing the masks displayed in local museums.

Masks or their equivalents were used to express a huge range of ritual and symbol. Among the Yoruba, dancers taking part in some ancestor cults wore masks which covered the face, while others used complete head-pieces. Others still had costumes with no sculptured mask at all—many of the forest peoples of the Ivory Coast painted their faces in brilliant colours and their upper torsos white, while dressing the rest of their bodies in fibre costumes. Masks were made to influence and contact spirits, whether ancestor spirits or spirits of animals and plants. Some people were in-different to their masks, or actually disliked them, but as they pleased the spirits they put up with them.

In some instances the masks, although worn, were not even meant to be seen by the people participating in the ceremony. The masks of the Kalabari people of the Nigerian forests represented a water spirit with human and hippopotamus features, and were worn on top of the dancer's

head so that the main features of the sculpture faced the sky. An elaborate ruff hid the masks from the spectators, for the dance was directed towards the spirit, not towards man. In fact, the Kalabari regarded the sight of the masks with a surprising apathy—even when the spirit was being invoked—if not with downright revulsion. Pregnant women were advised not to look at some sculpture 'lest their children acquired its big eyes and long nose, and so be born ugly'.

Among the Senufo, Baule and Anyi peoples of the Ivory Coast the mask was a channel of communication with Go, the Supreme Being, through the mediation of the ancestor spirits. The power of the mask to influence the ancestors depended on the social prestige of the owner, since a man could only reach prominence with their help, and his very success showed that the ancestors favoured him. An inherited mask retained its power over the ancestors, and the more prestigious its owner was in this life, the more powerful he would be as an ancestor spirit.

The use of all masks amongst the Ivory Coast peoples was regulated by the high priest of Go. His house contained not only the potent symbol which was the source of his power, but the actual presence of the ancestors, for it was in his hut that prominent people were buried and their masks preserved. These masks were of the highest rank, followed by masks upon which heads of families sacrificed to their ancestors. Next came avenging masks, which acted as police and judiciary combined, then initiation masks, and finally teaching, informing and entertaining masks. Some masks were considered to be the materialization of spirits which lived in the forest or bush, and revealed themselves because they wished to take part in the life of human beings. Among the Iwobe of Ivory Coast there was a belief that a group of pure spirits, *kosri*, gave the laws of social organization to the first man, and that these laws separated man from the animals. Each law was symbolized by a great mask made to resemble the spirit which gave it.

The masks of the Iwobe never represented a woman's face. They were symbols of virility, because it was a mask that lay at the origin of the differentiation of the sexes. At first the sexes were indistinguishable; then one group acquired the first mask from the kosri, and with it virility, together with superiority over the other group, which developed feminine characteristics.

At the same time, the first Iwobe men received the secret societies, which were already in two groups. One group drew its power from the ancestors, forming societies of great masks, the other from the kosri. Like all other West African peoples, the Iwobe used masks and dance as a representation of the universe, to express internal solidarity and self-sufficiency, and to express their difference from other communities.

Masks were designed to be seen in the movement of dance, perhaps in the flickering light of torches, and to be most effective when seen in violent motion with full costume. The Nigerian novelist, Chinua Achebe, comments upon this in *The Arrow of God*, describing a carver, Edogo. 'When he had finished carving the face and head he had been a little disappointed. But the owners of the work had not complained; in fact they had praised it very strongly. Edogo knew, however, that he must see the mask in action to know whether it was good or bad.'

Summoned by insistent drumming, masked figures would appear out of the forest; all were transformed in a world of magic, wonder, fear and awe. The role of the moon in these rituals was crucial. It was at full moon that secret dances were performed and the more violent rites took place. Sexual ceremonies were likely to be conditioned by the moon, for the state of ecstasy induced by masked dances was attributed to lunar influence, as that was the plane on which ghosts and spirits had their being.

By means of the public dance spectacular, barely perceived powers were made available to men of good standing within the community. The essence of life, of fertility, of sex, of deep-seated needs and desires, was summoned in the intensity of dance, allowing the people to experience

these powers and to cement the bonds of their society.

Initiation rituals drew upon these same forces so that the candidates would achieve a state of fusion with the generative process. Strictly speaking, initiation was into a secret society. But membership of a secret society was often an indication of adulthood, so joining a secret society was the same as becoming an adult. Moreover, the initiation ceremonies were organized and run by the secret societies. For a West African, to be a member of a group was like forming a link in an electrical circuit: as long as contact was maintained, the individual shared in the power generated by the group as a whole. For the individual to break the link, to become separate from the chain, spelt death—in many cases, not merely symbolic death. It was therefore necessary in initiating a young adult to seal the psyche indelibly with the impress of those ties which united the individual to the group.

The ceremonies by which this was achieved were highly dramatic; they were the equivalent to the voluntary death of the individual and his re-birth into the collective life of his people. This sense of collectivity induced a mental attitude which made itself apparent in every circumstance of life. It was the basis of an African's code of ethics that an individual action should be judged good or evil according to the effect it might have on the group.

When the day of initiation arrived, the candidates went into a series of frenzied dances whose movements were calculated to induce a state of ecstasy. Then, at the climax of the ceremony, came the dramatic act of circumcision. In some societies this was less a surgical operation than the infliction of genital wounds by a strange and fearful figure dressed as a leopard, who pounced unexpectedly from the cover of the bush.

The circumciser often came from the blacksmith caste. In order to reduce the risk of failure, or complications for the candidates, he and his assistants had to maintain absolute chastity for a period before and after the operation. They wore terrifying masks, to heighten the dramatic impact of the operation and so deepen the suffering which it entailed. This in its turn, by stirring into life psychic relationships previously unknown, and by unleashing the candidate's latent spiritual responses, effected the desired individual metamorphosis. His childhood clothes were burnt and he often received a new name, for the name contained the essence of the person.

The pain was intense. The candidates were made to sit in line, or in a circle, with their legs apart, while the iron surgical instrument of the circumciser was heated over a fire. An assistant held each candidate down in turn, as the circumciser approached holding the red-hot instrument. He pulled the prepuce forward with one hand and suddenly cut it off. Sometimes as a potion to ease the pain the candidates had to drink the water in which the instrument had been immersed; sometimes more effective analgesics were provided.

Similar rites were prescribed for women. Female circumcision did not always take the same forms amongst West African peoples, but it generally consisted of clitorectomy; sometimes there was cauterization rather than cutting. Normally a severe prohibition excluded all males from the chosen spot in the bush or forest clearing, although there were instances of an older man being present as an assistant. He lay on the ground beneath the girl, using his legs and arms in such a way that she was kept immobile and her legs forced wide apart. The operator then took hold of the clitoris with a pair of wooden pincers and cut it away with a knife held in her other hand. When the operation was finished, the other women approached and forced the girls to dance, regardless of the pain and loss of blood, in imitation of coition.

The specifically sexual character of these ceremonies, both male and female, reflects, again, the emphasis which all West African societies placed on procreation and fertility. Yet not all interpreted their rites in the same way. Among the Dogon, the male and female principle were held to coexist

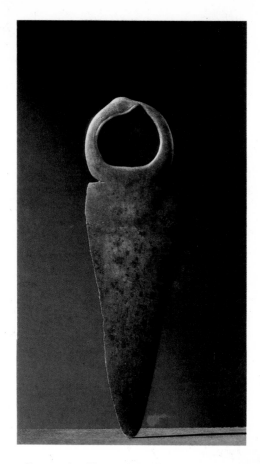

Above : An Akan cult knife used in circumcision rites or for tribal markings. Most Akan objects illustrate a saying or proverb. A bird looking backward is the visual equivalent of saying : 'To know where you are going, look from where you came.' In other words, recognize the past and you will have an inkling of what is in front of you.

Left : A dance headdress used by the Ekoi of the forests of eastern Nigeria. The Ekoi are well known for their skill in producing ultra-lightweight dance headdresses by stretching gazelle or monkey skin over a wooden frame.

On page 112 : A frightening magic medicine object used by the Fon of Dahomey. It is an accumulative sculpture, and so its magic power is equivalent to the total magic power of its many components.

in each individual at the moment of birth. The female principle in a man
was represented by the prepuce, and that of the male in a woman by the
clitoris. The act of initiation was thus a definite confirmation of the
individual's sex, the sign that he or she should from then on be considered
a fully adult male or female.

One legend has it that when the first man had recovered from his circumcision wound, he no longer wanted to have sexual intercourse with his
wife, because her vagina was not to his liking. The woman in desperation
went to their god and begged him to do to her as he had done to her
husband. In order to make her happy, the god cut away the apex of her
clitoris and her smaller labia. Thus the main stated reason for the practice
was to enhance aesthetic and physical pleasure—perhaps entirely from the
male point of view.

Clitorectomy was thought of not only as an aid to sexual intercourse, but
also as favouring motherhood, and as having magic powers. The Bambara
(a Mande-speaking people who lived near the Dogon) believed that any
man who had sex with an uncircumcised woman risked being 'punctured
by the dart' (the clitoris) and thus faced certain death.

The Asante called the male principle transmitted through the paternal
line *ntoro*, and the female principle transmitted through the maternal line
abrusua. Both principles co-existed in every human being, and both were
objects of special cults; offerings to ntoro were placed in a special bronze
vessel. These vessels, of most intricate design, were also used to hold gold-
dust, a representation of kingly power and one of the basic trade goods
upon which the commonwealth of Asante depended.

In many of the societies which developed centralized states the divine
kings had to expiate the collective sins of their people. Every Thursday in
Asante the asantehene, attended by courtiers and the members of his

116

family, visited a part of his palace called the House of Spirits. There he filled his mouth with holy water from a ritual gold vessel called the Cup of Spirits, and spat it around him, saying, 'Life for me—health for my people!' This expiation by a king sometimes involved him in being a scapegoat, and in some societies it went as far as the king being ritually sacrificed at the first signs of physical decrepitude. The decline of the physical powers of the oba of Benin would bring a comparable decline in the people as a whole and, ultimately, be their ruin. In some instances, the king's wives and servants or slaves were sacrificed as well, so that he might be properly attended in the next world.

Those societies which did not develop as kingdoms nevertheless had their own methods of mediating with the spirit world. The Ibo, for example, were governed not by kings and chiefs, but by gods and ancestors. Supernatural forces continually impinged on their life, and had to be propitiated by appropriate prayers and sacrifices. The god Chukwa had created the visible universe, many of whose aspects—including the sun, the sky and the earth—existed on two levels, as matter and as spirits, or *alusi*. To the Ibo living near the river, the Niger was the king of the alusi, which were found among temporal as well as natural phenomena, for instance in the four days of the Ibo week.

Unlike Chukwa, who was always benevolent, the alusi were forces for

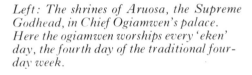

Left: The shrines of Aruosa, the Supreme Godhead, in Chief Ogiamwen's palace. Here the ogiamwen worships every 'eken' day, the fourth day of the traditional four-day week.

Right: A cast brass figure from the village of Tada on the Niger river in Nupeland, Nigeria. Possibly a figure of a hunter in ceremonial garb.

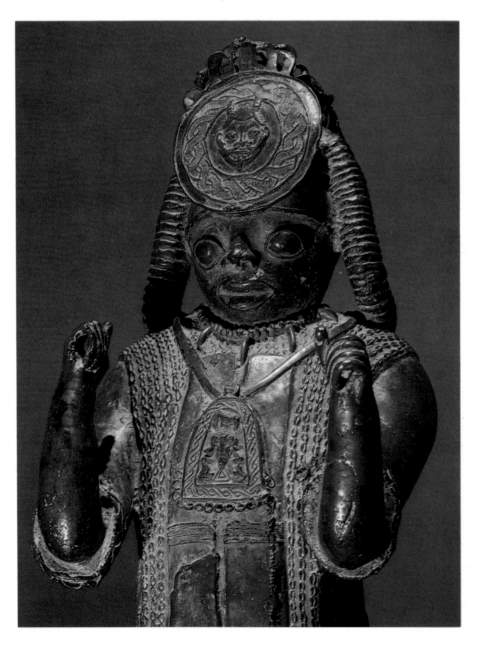

blessing or destruction, depending on circumstances. They punished social offenders and those who unwittingly infringed their privileges. Hence the key roles of the diviner, who interpreted the wishes of the alusi, and the priest, who placated them with sacrifice. There were different types of priest: the hereditary lineage priests, and priests who were chosen by particular gods for their service, after passing through a series of ascetic and mystical experiences.

Each village had its sacred places and particular divinities, which inhabited a sacred forest, rock, cave, or stream. And every individual had a *chi*, a personalized providence or spirit, which came from Chukwa and which reverted to him at the man's death. The chi might be well- or ill-disposed.

People who had lived well-spent lives, died in socially approved ways, and were given correct burial rites, became ancestor spirits and lived in any one of several worlds of the dead which all mirrored the one world of the living. They watched over the living, were periodically reincarnated among them, and were called 'the returners'. The living honoured them with sacrifices. Unhappy spirits who died bad deaths, and lacked correct burial rites, could not return to the world of the living, or enter that of the dead. They wandered homeless and dispossessed, expressing their grief by causing harm among the living.

Religious taboos, especially those surrounding priests and titled men, involved a great deal of asceticism. Whole communities deprived themselves of palatable and nutritious foods in religion's name—for instance, sacred fish. They expected, in return for prayers and sacrifices, blessings such as wealth, longevity and prosperity—and especially children, the greatest of blessings.

Certain Ibo beliefs sought to provide an explanation of imperfectly understood natural phenomena. There was, for instance, a wicked spirit who took the form of a beautiful child. He was frequently reborn in a family only to die, tormenting the unfortunate parents. This may have been an explanation of sickle-cell anaemia, which was common in Iboland: children born to apparently healthy parents who were carriers of the sickle-cell trait would usually die in infancy.

Their religion led the Ibo into some forms of apparent oppression and injustice. For instance, multiple births were regarded as typical of the animal world, so twins were considered less than human, and put to death (as were animals produced as single births); and the belief that the worlds of the dead mirror the world of the living encouraged the sacrifice of slaves at funerals, to serve the dead man in the life to come.

In most West African societies, the head of a family or lineage assumed a priestly role. He was expected to officiate at household religious ceremonies and to ensure that the god or ancestor was not alienated. When he died, he was usually succeeded by the person next in rank to him. In this case training was minimal; the new priest would be expected to be familiar with the likes and dislikes of his ancestor or god and to have watched and assisted at rituals performed by his predecessor.

Others were 'called' to the priesthood, and were believed to be in close communion with and have a deep-rooted understanding and knowledge of their god. Sometimes a child was set aside from birth to serve his or her god; this was a way in which the parents could give thanks to their particular god for a long-awaited child. More often a person was 'called' to the priesthood when he or she became possessed during a dance or ritual.

The Asante, for example, believed that when a person fell into a trance he was being chosen by his god. A priest or priestess interpreted the behaviour of the possessed person and usually said that the spirit of a particular god wished to 'marry' that person. After this he or she would probably become a novitiate priest. Sometimes this was a decision freely taken, sometimes the would-be priest needed considerable persuasion to take up the calling.

It was certainly not a decision to be taken lightly as the training period for a priest was three years and involved considerable self-denial. Married men and women had to leave their spouses during this period and sexual intercourse was forbidden. During the training period the novitiates lived with the priests who were training them. They were expected to show their devotion to their gods by adopting a frugal life-style: at night they slept in the god's temple, ate little, and fasted on the god's ceremonial days; they washed in cold water without soap and could not cut their hair.

Initiation into the rituals and the body of knowledge required by a priest was gradual. As the novices proved devotion to their gods, more secrets could be revealed to them. The secrets and skills of a priest could be very dangerous if misused, for the spirit world was often capricious. A priest who failed to understand or interpret correctly the demands of his god could bring misfortune to his followers.

The training was intended to bring the novices into close communion with their gods. Special medicines containing several kinds of leaves were used in order to help them see their deity and to hear his voice. During the first year of training the novice had to undergo a ritual to bring him closer to the spirit world and the spirits of dead men. An Asante priest described the ritual as follows:

Below: Interior of the fetish room of Abirim shrine. Abirim is one of the many Asante spirit-medium shrines, of which all the mediums are priestesses.

'The instructing priest will collect leaves from any plant growing over some grave in the *samanpow* [thicket of the ghosts] and bring them to the village where they are placed in a pot. Eggs and a fowl are then sacrificed upon them, and the pot containing them is placed upon

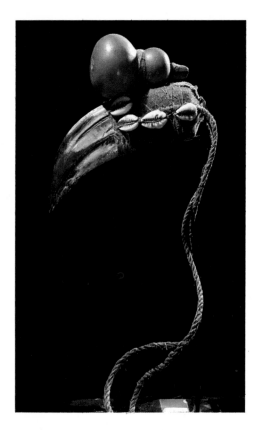

Above: A medicine object made from a hornbill's skull to which a calabash or gourd is attached, and this contains medicine (meaning magic). A similar kind of medicine or voodoo is common to the West Indies as part of the beliefs and cults introduced there by African slaves.

the grave from which the leaves were taken. The novice is then ordered to go alone in the middle of the night to the samanpow and "bathe" with the medicine in this pot. The ghosts will beat him and you will hear him screaming, but he must "bathe" nevertheless. Three times he must go to the grave for seven nights in succession, and "bathe" there.' (R. S. Rattray *Religion and Art in Ashante* London 1927, repr. 1959)

Having survived this ordeal, the trainee priest would, over the next two years, be taught how to use fetishes (*suman*) and how to divine the will of his god. He would be taught the taboos, or prohibitions, the god placed on his followers, and would observe them strictly. He would learn which spirits could be vengeful and which trees, animals or shrines they might come to rest in. He would learn also how to call up spirits and persuade them to enter shrines in the temple.

The priest was an important figure in sorcery. His knowledge of (and sometimes his ability to manipulate) the spiritual forces at work in every aspect of life was regarded as essential. Priests were often used by kings and chiefs as advisers, diviners and specialists in rituals.

In the kingdom of Oyo, for example, priests and diviners were found at every stage in the administrative hierarchy surrounding the alafin. Several members of the Council of State, the Oyo Mesi, had priestly functions as the leaders of cults dedicated to particular gods, such as Ogun, god of iron, and Oranyan, the legendary ancestor of the king.

The most powerful member of the Oyo Mesi was the *bashorun*. If a weak alafin was on the throne the bashorun could become the most powerful man in the land. He could exploit his position as 'diviner of the king's spiritual condition' to oust an unpopular or unworthy alafin. Every year he supervised a secret ritual which was intended to ascertain whether or not the alafin was on good terms with his spirit double or *orun*. The bashorun's divination might indicate that the king was on bad terms with his spirit double and this meant that some misfortune would befall the kingdom. A sacrifice might appease the spirit double, but in rare cases the state of the alafin's spiritual condition was such that rejection became unavoidable.

The alafin, the Oyo Mesi and the Ogboni secret society represented the three most powerful political elements within Oyo: the alafin symbolized the sky, the Ogboni the earth and the Oyo Mesi mankind. The Ogboni cult was the most awesome in the kingdom. The earth spirit was as old as Olorun, the Supreme God, and therefore not one of his subjects. The Ogboni were therefore independent of other gods, and their supernatural powers were greatly feared. It was believed that anyone who revealed the secrets of Ogboni rites would die by magic.

Most Yorubas assumed that the main function of the Ogboni was judicial. In fact, their secret role as ritual specialists of the alafin and as the mediators between him and the Oyo Mesi was more important:

'When a king died they were summoned to the palace, and after the corpse had been washed they were given its head and cleaned the flesh from the skull. During his installation the succeeding alafin was taken . . . to sacrifice to Shango and was given a dish containing the heart of his predecessor which he had to eat. Later he was taken to the Ogboni shrine, where the senior priest, the Oluwo, handed him the skull of his predecessor, which had been filled with a corn gruel for him to drink. This rite was said to open his ears to distinguish truth from falsehood, gave his words compelling power, and assigned to him alone the authority to execute criminals and his enemies at home and to make war on enemies abroad.' (R. Morton-Williams, 'The Yoruba Kingdom of Oyo' in Forde & Kaberry eds. *West African Kingdoms in the Nineteenth Century* London 1971)

Ritual and divination were not used only on important occasions. The

Right : A lower Niger pectoral with magical attachments. The suspended brass medicine bottle is a late Benin casting.

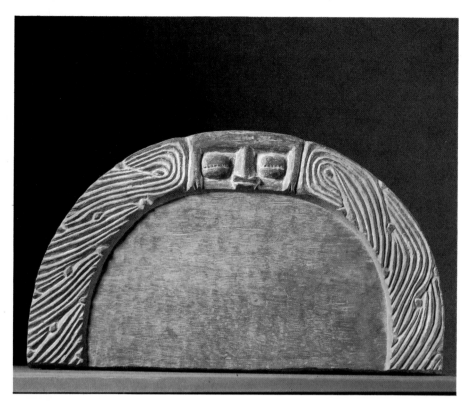

Left : A wooden board (only half is seen here) used by Yoruba priests or medicine-men for Ifa divination. Kola nuts are placed on sand on the board.

Below : Wooden baton used for Ifa divination. The baton would be used to tap the rim of a board like the one shown on the left. Divination not only looked into the future but also settled ordinary disputes in family and trade matters.

alafin could take few decisions without the approval of the gods. Diviners and priests were constantly on hand to communicate with the gods when a new palace official was appointed, when the alafin wanted to make changes in the administration or when an untoward event had happened.

The Fon people of Dahomey adopted the Yoruba system of divination known as Ifa, calling it Fa. Fon mythology relates that when the world was first created men had no knowledge of the gods. The Supreme Being sent two messengers to earth to show men Fa, the Word. This could be interpreted through divination, and thus they could learn their destiny, interpret events in the past and be instructed which gods to worship. One man was chosen to learn the secrets of divination, and this system, the Fon believed, was handed down through the generations to all diviners.

The king of Dahomey, like the alafin of Oyo, consulted diviners before he made any official appointments. The royal diviners were expected to find out whether these appointments had the approval of the king's ancestors. But priests and diviners in Dahomey had less sway over the king than did the priests and diviners of Oyo. All power was invested in the king and, although there was considerable freedom of religious thought, the activities of national cults were closely controlled by the state. No priest could be elected to a major cult without the king's approval; those who were chosen were known to be loyal supporters of the king, and the most powerful national cults were those linked to the royal lineage.

In the last resort, the culture and way of life of the peoples of West Africa were profoundly mysterious and were approached through mystery. Reality—the life cycles of men and women, and their physical environment—was more, much more than was immediately apparent. Everyday occurrences—the evidence of the senses—were transmitted continually into spiritual entities. The process was cyclical: the spirit world was ever being transmitted into the material. The meaning of life, in hard, concrete terms, not merely in philosophical abstractions, was always larger than the individual or the group. It encompassed the living and the dead, the animate and the inanimate, yesterday, today and tomorrow. The meaning of life was mysterious and was being approached constantly through the mysteries of cult, dance, mask, ritual, design and pattern. It was what gave life its zest, its vigour, its vitality and virility, its humour, and yet it was

Right : A brass rattle used in the rites of the secret Ogboni society of the Yoruba Ojo empire. These rattles are used to call on the ancestral spirits and ensure that they are present.

ever elusive. The West African past is rapidly becoming—if it has not already become—a lost past, merely a part of history. The elusiveness and the sense of loss is captured fleetingly in a poem by Gabriel Okara, a modern Nigerian poet, who shall have the last word:

The mystic drum beat in my inside
and fishes danced in the rivers
and men and women danced on land
to the rhythm of my drum

But standing behind a tree
with leaves around her waist
she only smiled with a shake of her head.

Still my drum continued to beat,
rippling the air with quickened
tempo compelling the quick
and the dead to dance and sing
with their shadows—

But standing behind a tree
with leaves around her waist
she only smiled with a shake of her head.

Then the drum beat with the rhythm
of the things of the ground
and invoked the eye of the sky
the sun and the moon and the river gods—
and the trees began to dance,
the fishes turned men
and men turned fishes
and things stopped to grow—

But standing behind a tree
with leaves around her waist
she only smiled with a shake of her head.

And then the mystic drum
in my inside stopped to beat—
and men became men,
fishes became fishes
and trees, the sun and the moon
found their places, and the dead
went to the ground and things began to grow.

And behind the tree she stood
with roots sprouting from her
feet and leaves growing on her head
and smoke issuing from her nose
and her lips parted in her smile
turned cavity belching darkness.

Then, then I packed my mystic drum
and turned away; never to beat so loud any more.

(Gabriel Okara, 'The Mystic Drum', in G. Moore and U. Beir (eds.)
Modern Poetry from Africa Harmondsworth 1973)

Acknowledgements

Werner Forman and the publishers would like to acknowledge the help of the following museums and private collections in permitting the photography shown on the pages listed:

Allan Brandt, New York: 50. The Trustees of the British Museum, London: 12 bottom, 15, 20, 41, 45, 46, 47, 51, 55, 77, 81, 98, 99, 101 top and bottom, 111, 121. Lance Entwistle: 40, 76. Friede Collection, New York: 91, 107. Fuhrman Collection, New York: 63. Philip Goldman Collection: title page, 123; ex-Philip Goldman Collection: 43. Ben Heller, New York: 112–13, 120. Toby Jack: 35 top. Koninklijk Museum voor Midden-Afrika – Musée Royal de L'Afrique Centrale, Tervuren, Belgium: 23, 72 right, 92, 106. W. Münsterberger: 8. Musée National, Niamey: 11 top, 57, 58 bottom, 59 top, 61. National Museum, Lagos: 11 bottom, 104, 105, 117. Museum of Natural History, New York: 79. Pace Gallery, New York: 82, 110. Private Collections: 12 top, 18, 21, 60, 75, 109, 115, 122 bottom. Charles Ratton, Paris: 48–9. ex-Herbert Rieser Collection: 83, 94. Harald Rome, New York: 74. Gustave Schindler, New York: contents page, 25, 69. Tishman Collection, New York: half-title page, 42, 85, 100, 114. Van Bussen Collection, The Hague: 108. Museum für Völkerkunde, Berlin: 32, 34, 35 bottom, 59 bottom, 62, 72 left, 122 top. Wallace Collection: 52.

Werner Forman would also like to thank the following for their assistance:

Mr Amegatcher, Accra; Nana Amonu X, Omanhene of Anomabu; Dr G.T. Anim, Accra; K.A. Brobey, Accra; Mohammed Mainasara Bungudu, Sokoto; Mr C. Descamps, Dakar; Mr C.K. Dufu, Accra; Dr A. Ferral, Niamey; Mr Alhasan Isaka, Kumasi; Prof. Krieger, Berlin; Prof. Maesen, Tervuren; Prof. R.B. Nunoo, Accra; Chief Okonghae Ogiamwen, Benin; Sultan Ibrahim Dumaroi, Agades; John Picton, London; Dr Angelika Rumpf, Berlin; Huguette Van Geluwe, Tervuren.

Bibliography

Ajayi, J.F.A. and Crowder, M. (Eds.) *History of West Africa* vol. 1, 2nd ed. (Longman, Harlow, Essex 1976; Columbia University Press, New York 1976)

Bovill, E.W. *The Golden Trade of the Moors* revised by R. Hallett (Oxford University Press, London 1970)

Crowder, M. *The Story of Nigeria* 4th ed. (Faber, London 1978)

Davidson, B. *Old Africa Rediscovered* (Gollancz, London 1959)

Egharevba, J.U. *A Short History of Benin* 3rd ed. (Ibadan University Press, Ibadan 1960)

Fage, J.D. *A History of West Africa* (Cambridge University Press, London and New York 1969)

Fagg, W. *Divine Kingship in Africa* (British Museum, London 1970)

Forde, D. and Kaberry, P.M. (Eds.) *West African Kingdoms in the Nineteenth Century* (Oxford University Press, London 1971)

Fraser, D. (Ed.) *African Art as Philosophy* (Interbook Inc., New York 1974)

Hopkins, A.G. *An Economic History of West Africa* (Longman, Harlow, Essex 1973; Columbia University Press, New York 1976)

Law, R.C.C. *The Oyo Empire c.1600–c.1836* (Clarendon Press, Oxford 1977)

Levtzion, N. *Ancient Ghana and Mali* (Methuen, London 1973)

Mauny, R. *Tableau géographique de l'Quest africain au moyen âge* (I.F.A.N., Dakar 1961)

Rattray, R.S. *Ashanti* (Clarendon Press, Oxford 1923)

Smith, R. *Kingdoms of the Yoruba* 2nd ed. (Methuen, London 1976)

Trimingham, J.S. *A History of Islam in West Africa* (Oxford University Press, London 1970)

Wilks, I. *Asante in the Nineteenth Century* (Cambridge University Press, Cambridge 1975)

Willett, F. *Ife in the History of West African Sculpture* (Thames & Hudson, London 1967)

Willis, J.R. (Ed.) *Studies in West African Islamic History* vol. 1: *The Cultivators of Islam* (Cass, London 1979)

Index

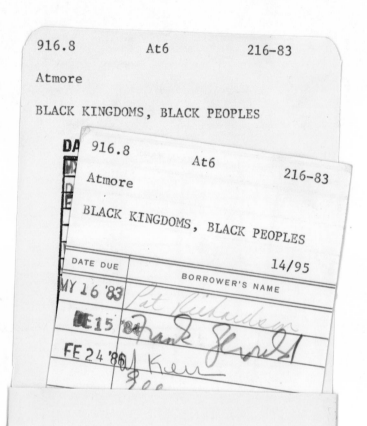

916.8   At6   216-83

Atmore

BLACK KINGDOMS, BLACK PEOPLES

916.8   At6   216-83

Atmore

BLACK KINGDOMS, BLACK PEOPLES

14/95

DATE DUE	BORROWER'S NAME
MY 16 '83	Pat Richardson
DE 15 '84	Frank Shields
FE 24 '86	Kerr
	$.00

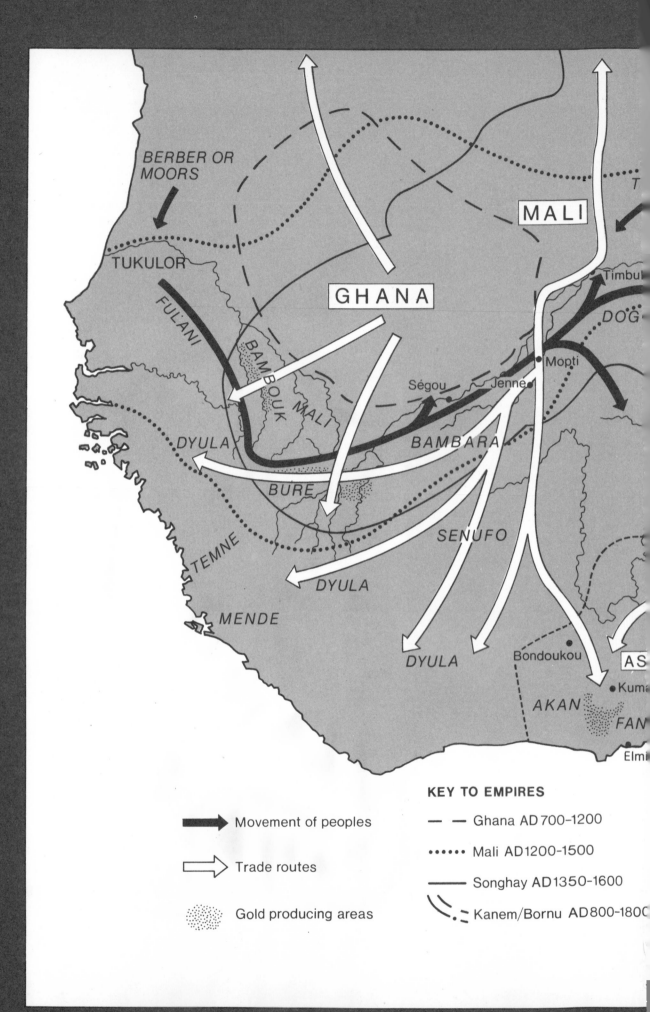

BERBER OR
MOORS

MALI

T

GHANA

TUKULOR

FULANI

BAMBOUK

DOG

MALI

Timbu

Ségou

Mopti

Jenne

DYULA

BAMBARA

BURE

SENUFO

TEMNE

DYULA

MENDE

DYULA

Bondoukou

AS

AKAN

Kuma

FAN

Elmi

KEY TO EMPIRES

➡ Movement of peoples

⇨ Trade routes

⋮⋮⋮ Gold producing areas

– – Ghana AD 700–1200

•••• Mali AD 1200–1500

—— Songhay AD 1350–1600

–·– Kanem/Bornu AD 800–1800